Conflict in Congress

Conflict in Congress

A Call for Moderation

Scot Schraufnagel

LEXINGTON BOOKS
Lanham • Boulder • New York • London

Published by Lexington Books
An imprint of The Rowman & Littlefield Publishing Group, Inc.
4501 Forbes Boulevard, Suite 200, Lanham, Maryland 20706
www.rowman.com

86-90 Paul Street, London EC2A 4NE

Copyright © 2024 by The Rowman & Littlefield Publishing Group, Inc.

All rights reserved. No part of this book may be reproduced in any form or by any electronic or mechanical means, including information storage and retrieval systems, without written permission from the publisher, except by a reviewer who may quote passages in a review.

British Library Cataloguing in Publication Information Available

Library of Congress Cataloging-in-Publication Data Available

ISBN: 978-1-66694-034-3 (cloth : alk. paper)
ISBN: 978-1-66694-035-0 (ebook)

∞™ The paper used in this publication meets the minimum requirements of American National Standard for Information Sciences—Permanence of Paper for Printed Library Materials, ANSI/NISO Z39.48-1992.

Contents

Acknowledgment		vii
Preface		ix
1	Legislative Conflict Theory	1
2	Measuring Conflict in Legislatures	19
3	Party Polarization and Member Incivilities: How Distinct Are the Two Dimensions of Conflict	43
4	What Explains Uncivil Member Behavior?	57
5	Measuring Legislative Productivity	71
6	Moderate Conflict and Legislative Productivity	85
7	Managing Conflict in Legislatures	107
Appendix A		123
Appendix B		129
References		131
Index		141
About the Author		147

Acknowledgment

There are many students and colleagues, throughout the years, who have played important roles in helping me think carefully about legislative conflict. I will not try to list them all here. I base this decision on my heartfelt and steadfast desire to make sure that I in no way dilute the extraordinarily important influence of Lawrence C. Dodd to my academic career and the development of arguments contained in this book. Professor Dodd, who was an associate of Robert Dahl, was writing about the importance of norms to reign in severe legislative conflict in the 1970s. When I first met Larry, in 1998, and shared some of my thinking about two-dimensional conflict in Congress, he suggested we work together. The level of incivilities or relational conflict in Congress had not yet peaked, and congressional scholars who reviewed our early work regarded our notions regarding legislative conflict, and the value of moderate conflict, with a healthy dose of skepticism. The concern was that relational conflict or incivilities and party polarization were inextricably linked and that even if they were theoretically distinct, there were likely no unique implications. Moreover, many imagined that relational conflict was impossible to measure reliably. These concerns were and are important. Unwaveringly, Professor Dodd encouraged me to continue developing the Legislative Conflict Theory elaborated in this book. In the very recent phone conversations I have had with Larry, he continues to encourage me. I am eternally grateful. Quite simply this book and the research it contains would not exist if not for the many long conversations Professor Dodd and I have had about legislative process, held over the phone, at academic conferences, and over lunch in Gainesville, Florida.

Preface

CONFLICT THEORIES

The goal of this book is to promote effective legislative process, and the spotlight is on legislative conflict in the U.S. Congress. The more general topic of societal conflict is an important preface to the study I am undertaking. Notably, when others discuss societal conflict, there are normally political implications. Classic political philosophers from Aristotle to St. Augustine, Age of Enlightenment thinkers such as Thomas Hobbes and Niccolo Machiavelli, and also Karl Marx and Friedrich Engels have all addressed sociopolitical conflict. In these great works, which span more than two millennia, there is a consensus that societal conflict is inevitable. Aristotle recognizes the normative value of social conflict, and he imagines lasting disagreement and social rivalries to be a vital part of how human beings live well together in successful political life (Skultety 2009). In *The City of God*, St. Augustine (1950 [426]) outlines two spiritual powers, faith and unbelief, which he holds have contended with each other since the fall of the angels. He concurred that conflict between good and evil will be with us forever, although he is clearly cheering for the "City of God" (faith) and would like to see it win out over the "City of Man" (unbelief) and for conflict to disappear.

Thomas Hobbes, writing in the seventeenth century, during England's Civil War, also sees conflict as inevitable. Specifically, he saw conflict occurring as the result of the equality found in the "state of nature." Hobbes argues that discord between individuals occurs because of "competition," "distrust," and the pursuit of "glory" (Hobbes 1991 [1651]). Unlike Aristotle, Hobbes philosophizes that conflict is problematic and a threat to self-preservation and suggests the need for a sovereign political authority to manage conflict, lest life be nasty, brutish, and short (Hobbes 1991, Chapter 13). Niccolo

Machiavelli (1998 [1532]) also recognizes the need for effective leadership to help manage the inevitability of conflict. Of course, Machiavelli's competent leaders may not be "good people," which creates consternation for many with his political philosophy. His premise, with respect to personal virtue, is that leaders (princes) who act in accordance with virtue can be harmful to the state or government.

Perhaps no one thought more carefully about societal conflict than Karl Marx and Friedrich Engels (1998 [1848]). In their view, conflict is perpetual because of competition for scarce resources. Marx refers to his ideas as "Conflict Theory," and his thinking is not entirely distinct from some Enlightenment thinkers in that each suggests one maintains social order via coercion rather than consensus or conformity. Marx and Engels see society divided along lines of economic class and that the ruling class will use social and economic institutions to maintain their dominance. Conflict is between the economic elite and the working class (proletariat). This view is somewhat problematic for a contemporary analysis of legislative conflict, because, normally, competing elites (capitalists) define the nature of conflict in modern legislatures around the world. Notably, later versions of Marx's Conflict Theory do recognize conflict among capitalist factions (Malecki 1981), precisely as exists in the U.S. Congress today.

I am not intending this brief overview of some classic Western philosophy to slight the important writings on conflict by The Buddha, Confucius, and Avicenna. Each of these Eastern philosophers has made outstanding contributions to our understanding of sociopolitical conflict. Rather, my intention with this preliminary discussion of social conflict is to communicate to my reader that I am fully aware that I am treading on hollow ground when I discuss legislative conflict. I am not naïve. Great thinkers from all backgrounds have been thinking about conflict very carefully for ages. Likely, the only thing novel about this book, and the analysis of conflict contained within, is the specific organization of the discussion of sociopolitical conflict. In addition, I will provide several original empirical tests of a specific conflict theory. The hope is that the reader will see my approach as innovative and that the scrutiny will contribute to a better understanding of effective legislative process.

Considering contemporary discussions of conflict theory, it is imperative to note the work of organizational scholars who try to imagine the most effective way to manage the private-sector workplace (Bernard et al. 1957). Much of their focus is on conflict management. Some see people involved in conflict situations as troublemakers and explicitly note that business managers, when confronted with workplace conflict, need to enhance the collaborative spirit of the organization through the development of new norms that will change organizational culture (Blake and Mouton 1964; Likert and Likert 1976). Others consider conflict as natural and the source of new ideas and necessary to enhance workplace productivity and keep pace with a dynamic business environment. Louis Pondy (1967) suggests that conflict "may be functional as well as dysfunctional for the individual and the organization" (298). He holds that one should approach conflict resolution "with caution," so as not to suppress or squander innovation opportunities.

I offer this brief sketch of the work of organization scholars because their work has provided me considerable insights regarding conflict management in the congressional workplace. I will return to the work of these scholars in chapter 1 to make my thinking about two-dimensional legislative conflict more explicit. I initially thought my consideration of the two dimensions of legislative conflict, one policy-oriented and the other based on personal relations, was novel. Upon investigation, I learned that organizational scholars have recognized my insights and have been writing about them for some time. I first encountered the notion of two-dimensional workplace conflict when reading the work of Karen Jehn (1997). She labels the first type of disagreement "task conflict" and the second "relational conflict."

Jehn argues that high levels of task conflict need low levels of relational conflict to be productive. Others note, specifically, that "task conflict is widely believed to be beneficial whereas relationship conflict is destructive" (Jiang, Zhang, and Tjosvold 2013, 714). However, Jiang and colleagues (2013) concur with Jehn when noting that for task conflict to be productive organizations need "individuals skilled in emotion regulation" to limit the negative influence of relationship conflict (714). Considering individuals skilled in emotion regulation, in the context of the U.S. Congress, we might note members committed to legislative norms that promote civil deliberations (Alexander 2021). According to Jehn (1997), "norms" or adherence to norms can rein in high-task conflict. I hold that the difference in policy preferences, in Congress, is analogous to task conflict in the private-sector workplace and that civility norms can help rein in unbridled policy or "task" conflict. Alexander (2021), for his part, argues that legislative norms are dynamic and can compete with one another in terms of conflict management (chapter 7).

Stepping back, it is commonly understood that social science theories can be descriptive, prescriptive, or both. For instance, Rational Choice Theory (RCT) refers to a set of guidelines, largely based on rational actor self-interest, and the "invisible hand," which helps us understand economic and social behavior (Smith 1985 [1776]). The "invisible hand" element of the theory, which is a metaphor for the unseen forces of self-interest, is essentially descriptive, suggesting this is how things are, whether we like it or not. One can view the "rational actor" element of RCT as both descriptive and prescriptive. People are rational and ought to behave rationally. Importantly, scholars criticize the rational actor aspect of RCT because it claims to be instrumental, or the most important thing causing something to happen.

Critics of RCT note that rational actors disagree about what is best; hence, RCT cannot be instrumental (Boudon 1998; Hindmoor 2011). Moreover, some view the "self-interest" element of RCT as justifying greed or selfishness and the prescriptive value of RCT takes a hit (Christiano 2004). Still others note Adam Smith's focus on self-interest, when he first formulated RCT, was about self-preservation and did not involve materialism (works cited in Stabile 1997). If this is correct, the theory becomes more justifiably prescriptive, again. All this is to suggest that there can be a jumbling of the descriptive and prescriptive elements of social science theory.

In this book, I introduce Legislative Conflict Theory (LCT). I will try to be as explicit as possible about the descriptive and prescriptive aspects of the theory, although there is likely to be some muddling. To begin, LCT suggests legislative conflict is two-dimensional and the intention of this aspect of the theory is to be descriptive. That is, I suggest both dimensions of conflict always exist in all groups, and democratically elected legislatures are no exception. LCT also suggests moderate legislative conflict is best. Not too high and not too low. This aspect of the theory I intend to be prescriptive. I gain many of my insights about the value of moderate conflict from Robert Dahl (1967). Dahl, in his treatise on pluralist democracy, recognizes the value of conflict in legislatures and his primary concern is that conflict not be too "severe" (270–79).

I am imagining that combining the insights of Dahl and organizational scholars may be unique, and perhaps therein lies my contribution. Yet, the long history of scholarly attention to societal conflict leaves me humbled. Certainly, my focus on legislative conflict is not original. Much previous scholarship that discusses legislative conflict focuses on conflict between the executive and legislative branches of government (Peterson and Greene 1994), while others discuss legislative conflict in terms of an adept legislative process. For instance, Taeko Hiroi and Lucio Renno (2014) discuss managing the cohesiveness of coalition governments in multi-party systems to attenuate obstructionism and produce a more competent legislative process (357). I embrace and welcome their concern for effective lawmaking and will show in this book how the productivity of the U.S. Congress has waxed and waned over the past 100 years. Specifically, with a new indicator of Topical Legislative Productivity, I will show that the second decade of the twenty-first century experiences waning effectiveness. This is concerning. Although the focus of the book is squarely on theory development as it relates to legislative productivity, as is the case with Hiroi and Renno (2014), the broader concern for regime stability is not lost on me.

Last, it is important that I be transparent about my own philosophical bend. I engage in naturalist thinking, or the notion that there is great value in the scientific method and that one obtains knowledge through scientific investigation. Moreover, I am a humanist and believe that people have an ethical responsibility to lead lives that contribute to the greater good. However, my take on humanism is not wholly consistent with the views of the American Humanist Association.[1] For instance, I am not antithetical to religion, and consider myself a theist. Next, I am utilitarian (Mill 2003 [1859]) and adhere to the doctrine that actions are right if they are useful or for the benefit of the majority. I also have a positivist bend, holding that we can verify rationally justifiable assertions mathematically. I know this is a lot. Yet, this is my background, and these beliefs define the parameters for the inquiries I present in this book. A "more perfect union" defines my base motivation.

NOTE

1. American Humanist Society, https://americanhumanist.org/what-is-humanism/edwords-what-is-humanism/ (last accessed September 12, 2023).

Chapter 1

Legislative Conflict Theory

In the summer of 2020, violent protests took place in cities throughout the United States in response to the murder of George Floyd by police officers in Minneapolis, Minnesota. In Portland, Oregon, there were nightly rallies, which included considerable vandalism to federal buildings including the Federal Court House. Then, in January 2021, a group tried to sabotage the counting of Electoral College votes in the nation's Capitol, to create chaos and disrupt the orderly transition of presidential authority. Congress was under attack. This is the backdrop for this book on legislative conflict. In the United States, citizens on the left and right are both unsatisfied with the present state of political affairs. Notably, each group is decidedly well-armed and neither seems to feel they have an effective voice in the governing process. Individuals from both ends of the ideological spectrum, in recent years, have resorted to violence as a means of political communication.

Moreover, the public's approval of Congress, in the contemporary era, is typically abysmal. Threats of government shutdowns as a result of legislative stalemate are commonplace. These risks frustrate economic markets both at home and around the world. Pressing issues such as climate change, healthcare cost, immigration reform, and gun violence routinely go unaddressed by the national legislature in the United States. When action does occur, it is generally piecemeal. It is not my intention, in this chapter, to make the case that things are "worse than ever." Certainly, the nineteenth and twentieth centuries experienced their own extraordinary circumstances, perhaps greater than what we face, today. Civil War in the nineteenth century and the World Wars in the twentieth century are stark reminders of chaos throughout U.S. history. Yet, the only era we can do anything about is the future, and current events help to express the parameters of actionable items.

Considering the violence in 2020, and early 2021, the third decade of the twenty-first century faces considerable challenges. The largest land war in Europe, since World War II, is taking place in Ukraine. With nuclear arsenals in play, mutually assured destruction defines the parameters of the war in Eastern Europe. The Middle East remains volatile, and conflict between Jews and Arabs is salient again, following an outbreak of often-indiscriminate violence against Israelis, in the fall of 2023, by Hamas a Palestinian paramilitary group. The Israeli Defense Forces' response has been less than measured. Often, the victims are innocent civilians. To be certain, there is no easy fix, which causes many to, figuratively, throw up their arms incredulously. With sociopolitical problems of great consequence, some of the most civic-minded people simply try to ignore.

Well-intentioned reformers, in the U.S., depending on their ideological bend, do grapple with changes to election laws, redistricting processes, judicial ethics, or limits on government's authority as ways to address systemic chaos. Yet, one must wonder if there might be a more wide-ranging consideration or solution. Is there something fundamentally wrong that a more complete understanding of sociopolitical conflict can address? I hold there is. Specifically, I suggest that all people, and especially governing elites, need a better appreciation of the essential character of conflict. If we can develop a better appreciation of the nature of social discord, we can perhaps then begin to formulate comprehensive solutions to violence and mayhem. Moreover, I believe it is prudent to start with legislatures.

If we are to experience peace and prosperity in democratic settings, it is essential for legislatures to function effectively. To this end, I introduce Legislative Conflict Theory (LCT) as a means to understand more completely the essential nature of sociopolitical conflict. In this treatise, my focus and testing ground is the U.S. Congress. This is not to suggest that this is the most important place to start. Instead, I start with Congress because it is the institution most familiar to me. My hope is that follow-up research will focus on other legislative bodies, state and local in the United States, but also governing institutions in other countries. If my suspicions have merit, LCT could foster a better understanding of government dysfunction the world over.

LCT is both descriptive and prescriptive. Importantly, LCT does not view political conflict as either good or bad. In fact, I will argue that it can be both. The descriptive element of LCT holds that political conflict is two-dimensional and that the value of political conflict will depend on which dimension one is considering and the context in which it is occurring.[1] Defining the two dimensions of legislative conflict, precisely, is challenging. Yet, defining dense concepts is what social scientists do. In broad terms, I hold that differences in opinion about the material world, and corresponding policy preferences, characterize the first dimension of legislative conflict. The second dimension entails a commitment to civility and an appreciation of shared goals and objectives. I will be more precise.

In the context of Congress, I believe, one can capture the first dimension by considering the concept of political party polarization. I will consistently use this label. Most specifically, I am referring to the opposing policy positions of partisan actors. When the number of policy issues that partisan opponents disagree on grows, and co-partisans are homogeneous in their policy preferences, this fuels party system polarization. In other words, if there is little or no overlap in the policy preferences of competing partisans, party polarization is high. Importantly, this first dimension does not include the phenomenon of partisan opponents forsaking their true policy preferences and disagreeing with their opponents out of spite. The assumption here is that policy differences are real, heartfelt, and not reactionary. Scholars routinely capture party polarization with the roll call votes cast by members of the two major political parties with representation in the U.S. Congress.

The second dimension of legislative conflict is about individuals being unable to get along with one another on a personal level. I refer to this second dimension of legislative conflict as relational conflicts, incivilities, personalities, and norm breaking. I will use the terms interchangeably throughout the book. The second dimension of legislative conflict is higher when members of Congress (and the public) flout norms of deference, courtesy, and reciprocity. Although incivilities and relational conflict might always seem inappropriate, my take is that at times ramping up conflict, even incivilities, may be necessary. For instance, in authoritarian settings it is quite common for legislators to serve only to legitimize the chief executive or ruling oligarchy. Under this scenario, there is little in the way of useful dissension or conflict and some rabble-rousing incivilities might be a welcome respite to the collusion and indifference, which likely defines legislative processes.

Importantly, I suggest that the second dimension is not the same as what some refer to as "affective polarization" or the negative feelings that people have toward an opposing political party (Mason 2016; Rogowski and Sutherland 2016). Relational conflict and affective polarization relate in one obvious manner: they are both dense concepts that are difficult to measure systematically, especially with Congress-specific values. They are fundamentally different, however, in that, one is a feeling and the other is an overt action. People who get angry when they think about the opposing political party fuel affective polarization; this does not become norm-breaking incivilities until they act on those feelings. I think "affective polarization" has real potential to exacerbate both of the dimensions of legislative conflict I will be discussing. Yet, affective polarization is different in that it is more an emotional condition, and the two dimensions of conflict, discussed as part of LCT, are both behaviors. Moreover, both polarization and relational conflict can occur within a single party, without a partisan opponent as the target of the antagonism or annoyance. This further distinguishes each from affective polarization as scholars normally discuss the phenomenon.

A second aspect of LCT focuses on the need for moderate conflict, and this theoretical consideration is prescriptive. I do not use the term moderate to imply "low" conflict. Instead, the prescription is for some median level of conflict. This is the key element of LCT, and I will argue that the management of conflict at moderate levels will help to determine the extent to which our government serves its intended purposes. In other words, the government's ability to form a more perfect union, ensure domestic tranquility, provide for the common defense, and promote the general welfare will be dependent on the effective contestation of competing policy prescriptions at a median level. Some conflict is required to structure legislative debate. Once policy options and disagreements are established, members must accept the fact that political disagreement does not make an opponent our enemy, and both sides must move forward with civility and a commitment to courtesy and reciprocity.

It is not too difficult to imagine a low level of one dimension of legislative conflict working in tandem with a high level of the second dimension to produce moderate conflict. For instance, there may be highly polarized partisan actors working together in a civilized manner. Conversely, firebrands may shake loose idleness born of elite complicity. Either scenario may allow a legislature to address salient policy topics competently. Likewise, one can imagine moderate levels of both types of conflict. Now, there are some real and important policy differences and some healthy distrust of the opposition's motives, yet both sides are genuinely committed to the greater good. This mixture of conflict should also result in an effective legislative process. The management of overall conflict at some moderate level becomes an essential undertaking.

Much of the subsequent discussion, and ultimately all of the testing of LCT in this book, focuses on the U.S. Congress. Yet, it bears repeating, my contention is that the theory is applicable to legislative processes anywhere, even authoritarian settings, and at all levels of government in federal systems. The descriptive nature of two-dimensional legislative conflict and the prescriptive call for moderation should be relevant in any legislature, in any part of the world. Democratically elected legislatures certainly require conflict management, most immediately, to rein in factional passion. Legislatures in authoritarian settings likely need to ramp up conflict less they be complicit in the abuse of executive authority.

MORE ON LEGISLATIVE CONFLICT THEORY

From a normative perspective, legislative structures cannot operate effectively without well-defined conventions or norms of behavior (Dahl 1967,

277; Cooper 1970, Part IV). In this view, we elect representatives from within a conflict-ridden society precisely in order to represent those conflicts. Thus, they will generally bring to the legislature strong and even passionate feelings that reflect societal tensions, often elected precisely because they so accurately reflect factional passions. Members' special backgrounds and personalities will often shape the ways in which they express their feelings, with some members having developed a capacity for detachment while others will have volatile inclinations (Ross 1993; Cohen, Vandello, Puente, and Rantilla 1999). Whatever the case, human actors subject to the same passions and conflicts they are charged with mediating necessarily require guidance in understanding how to best regulate their own behavior in an effort to serve as responsible and effective mediators (Friedrich 1963, 302–14). Thus, a critical issue in the emergence of well-functioning legislatures is the construction and operation of relational norms (Matthews 1959; Polsby 1968).

The Madisonian structure of government was a committed attempt to address dual fears: an overly passive legislature, at one extreme, and an overly impassioned one, at the other. The intention was to ensure a well-functioning and activist Congress. Such a Congress would fulfill its mediating roles effectively while preventing conflict from surging out of hand. The Constitution thus gave Congress sufficient powers that factions would take it seriously as an arena for conflict mediation and pointed toward centralizing features such as the speakership and majority decision-making, both of which could help prompt policy action. Yet it also sought to create a general structural environment in ways that would constrain legislative passions. For instance, dividing Congress into two separate and roughly co-equal chambers, identifying circumstances that would require extra-majoritarian decision-making, and dispersing political power broadly among other branches and levels of government. Yet, the Constitution can only do so much. The Congress and the individuals who populate the institution must find a way forward in terms of constructing the internal organizational arrangements best suited to Congress fulfilling the role of conflict mediator (Dodd 1981, 416–18).

As with constitutional construction, the creation of internal organizational arrangements within a legislature must necessarily walk a fine line. They must facilitate principled and serious attention to the numerous conflictual sociopolitical issues at play in a mass society, so that these problems go recognized and debated in open and frank deliberations, even at the risk of provoking significant conflict within the legislature. Yet organizational arrangements must also help to moderate institutional conflict enough so that productive majority policymaking can eventually occur (Maass 1983; Bessette 1994). In constructing such arrangements, legislators must recognize that structures and norms which foster high conflict may be hostile to the functioning of a productive and responsive legislature. However, so can institutional arrangements or norms that allow for too little conflict.

To move forward in this attempt to understand two-dimensional conflict, and the promotion of moderate conflict, it is important that I communicate more carefully what I mean by "relational conflict," "personalities," or "norm-breaking incivilities." The intention is to understand why legislative norms, which promote civil discourse, are necessary. Even if those norms sometimes go too far in stifling meaningful policy debate. Importantly, conflict based on "personalities" has occurred throughout congressional history. Indeed, these clashes have often resulted in temper tantrums, pushing and shoving, and even more intense violent acts. To initiate a better understanding of this second dimension of legislative conflict, it may help to tell a few stories. Each story will ultimately be included in the measurement of relational conflict that I use in subsequent chapters.

UNDERSTANDING THE OTHER DIMENSION OF LEGISLATIVE CONFLICT

Shortly after five o'clock in the evening on September 3, 1890, it became clear there was an ongoing dispute between two Republican members of Congress. After most members had departed for the day, Representative Robert P. Kennedy of Ohio took the floor in the House of Representatives in front of a handful of listeners, seated on each side of the chamber, to harangue Senator Matthew Stanley Quay of Pennsylvania. He began discussing a bill to regulate Federal elections in the southern states, legislation that had stalled in the Senate due to the recommendation of Senator Quay. Kennedy stated, "The cloak of Senatorial courtesy has become a stench in the nostrils and a by-word in the mouths of all the honest citizens of the land. It makes a cloak behind which ignorant and arrogant wealth can purchase its way to power and then hide its cowardly head behind the shameless protection of Senatorial silence."[2]

Though these words took Kennedy beyond the boundaries of debate normally allowed in the Lower Chamber, the Representative continued his criticism by targeting Senator Quay, specifically, and personally. "The Judas Iscariot of 2,000 years ago is to find a counterpart in the Judas Iscariot of today. The Judas who took the thirty pieces of silver and went and hanged himself has left an example for the Matt Quays that is well worthy of their imitation."[3] In his closing, the Ohio representative called Quay "a branded criminal," and declared, "I denounce him."[4] Although there was a policy difference at the core of this conflictual episode, it was largely about personalities and the norm-breaking discourse is what I am labeling relational conflict.

In another instance, on February 22, 1902, the Senate gathered to perform its daily business, and to celebrate the birth of the country's first president, George Washington. Following the reading of Washington's Farewell Address by Senator Julius Caesar Burrows (R-MI), Benjamin Ryan Tillman (D-SC) took the floor to discuss the Philippine tariff bill. His remarks took the form of "a scathing review of the government's policy toward the Philippines," and drew responses from several members, including Senator John Coit Spooner (R-WI).[5] Tillman assailed the method used to prompt ratification of the treaty. He charged that William Jennings Bryan, though a Democratic leader, had traveled to Washington, D.C., to help the Republicans ratify the treaty and because he initially failed to secure enough votes he "found [it] necessary to get one vote by bribery."[6]

With this accusation, Senator Spooner pressed Tillman to reveal the name of the man who accepted the bribe. Tillman initially refused. After a short exchange, Senator Spooner persuaded the South Carolinian to reveal the person by name and Tillman noted it was none other than his colleague from the Palmetto State, a fellow Democrat, Senator John L. McLaurin (D-SC). Spooner, in response, sent a note to McLaurin who was attending a meeting of the committee on Indian Affairs. Upon arriving in the Senate chamber, McLaurin took his seat only two places from Tillman, with Senator Henry Moore Teller (D-CO) seated between them. Tillman rose to speak and delivered "one of the most vitriolic speeches ever heard in the Senate" according to the *Washington Post*.[7]

Twenty minutes later, McLaurin rose to a question of privilege and very calmly, as though he was going to make a speech about the national holiday, stood in the center aisle, and looking directly at the president of the Senate, reviewed the accusations so recently directed at him. Then turning halfway toward Tillman, McLaurin noted that Tillman's speech was full of deliberate, willful, and malicious lies. Up, like a flash, and "with the agility of a cat," Senator Tillman leaped over Senator Teller to where his colleague was standing, and with his left fist, he struck McLaurin on the forehead, just above the right eye.[8] McLaurin returned the blow and a skirmish ensued, both men repeatedly attempting to strike one another. After other members restrained them, the combatants made several additional attempts to renew the fisticuffs. The presiding officer closed the session to the public and cleared the gallery.

Though neither of these clashes, just elaborated, were the most brutal showdown to take place in Congress,[9] they are particularly good examples of the way that some senators and representatives have allowed their personal feelings to spill over into legislative debate. There have been numerous occasions in Congress when various members have yelled, planned for a duel, swung their fists, and even brandished weapons. Perhaps the most remarkable characteristic of the two tales, just mentioned, is the fact that the feuding men in each story belonged to the same political party. Nearly equally shocking, in the second story, is that Tillman and McLaurin were senators from the same state! The two Democrats represented the same constituency. Presumably, their duties required them to be capable of working together for the good of the people of South Carolina.

If conflict, in Congress, were only the result of partisan roll call differences, or affective polarization, what would drive two members of the *same* political party to attack each other verbally and, in the case of Tillman and McLaurin, physically? If the members were only interested in the passage (or failure) of pending legislation, it is doubtful that one would go so far as to assault a home-state colleague on the floor of the Senate. Moreover, and more directly, it is not difficult to imagine how outbursts and personal vindictiveness can compromise healthy legislative debate and a competent lawmaking process. Importantly, not all-relational conflict needs to reach the levels just described in order to help define the parameters of legislative conflict on a specific legislative day or in a particular legislative session. Allow me to provide some more examples.

Many congressional observers have heard about heated exchanges on the House and Senate floor during the colorful history of Congress. Some might be more surprised to learn that relational conflict in the form of verbal assaults, and physical altercations, have occurred throughout congressional history, and some of them quite recently. In 1985, Representative Thomas Downey (D-NY) grabbed Representative Robert Dornan (R-CA) by the shoulder and forcibly jerked him around. Dornan responded by grabbing Downey aggressively by the collar and necktie, threatening to do him bodily harm. Dornan later claimed he only wanted to straighten the knot in Downey's tie because "I like the members to look elegant on the floor, you know."[10] Downey, for his part, had taken exception to Dornan labeling him a "wimp" in a speech before the Conservative Political Action Conference.

In 1988, at the behest of Senate Majority Leader Robert C. Byrd (D-WV), Capitol Police literally dragged Senator Robert "Bob" Packwood (R-OR), feet first, into the Senate chamber to establish a quorum. Republicans had been hiding in the Capitol Building and in the nearby Senate office buildings to prevent a vote on campaign finance reform. Senator Arlen Specter (R-PN) suggested that

> The knock on the door and the forceful entry into Senator Packwood's office smack of Nazi Germany, smack of Communist Russia, but are hardly characteristic of the United States of America and should be even less characteristic of the operation of the United States Senate.[11]

What is particularly striking about Senator Specter's observation is that the events he describes *are*, in fact, characteristic of legislative processes in the United States at certain times. History is replete with incidents of general normlessness in Congress, and the modern era is no exception.

In July 2003, in the House of Representatives, it was the Democrats' turn to walk out. In this case, it was a committee hearing, and minority Democrats were objecting to changes made to a pension bill in the middle of the night. Left behind to monitor the proceedings, for the Democrats, was Representative Peter Stark (D-CA). His partisan colleagues had gone to a House library in protest and to make clear they did not support the late-night antics of the majority party and committee Chair Bill Thomas (R-CA). When Stark interjected his views on the proceedings, Representative Scott McInnis (R-CO) told him to "shut up." The *Congressional Record* suggests that Stark followed this pronouncement with the following statement, "Oh you think you are big enough to make me, you little wimp? Come on. Come on over here and make me. I dare you. You little fruitcake. You little fruitcake. I said you are a fruitcake." McInnis said he feared corporal harm from Stark who at age seventy-one was twenty-one years his senior.

Both the McInnis and Stark encounter and the Packwood affair were largely about the violation of legislative norms intended to promote the effective deliberation of pending legislation. In other words, the clashes were not the product of political disagreement over public policy options but instead were fights over intra-chamber legislative procedures. Neither of these battles featured healthy political debate of the important issues of our times; instead, the altercations were indicative of a blanket inability of colleagues in the congressional workplace to agree upon rules and get along with one another. Evidence, I suggest, of relational conflict.

The physical exchange between Dornan and Downey is also notable for its lack of political or partisan substance. It turns out the core of this encounter was personal. The two had battled two years prior, before Dornan was a member of Congress. At that time, Downey was part of an effort to block Dornan from receiving an appointed position in the Arms Control and Disarmament Agency. During their run-in on the House floor, Dornan referred to Downey costing him the job. Hence, each of the three altercations involved participants from opposing parties, but in none of these cases was the fight obviously political. The conflicts occurred largely because the participants did not like or, at a minimum, respect each other's position on a matter of procedure or personal preference. Differing philosophies of good governance or appropriate public policy was not the central issue. If they had been, the encounters would arguably be more tolerable from the standpoint of classic democratic theory. Political battles over policy preferences commonly define quality or competent democratic process (Dahl 1967, 270). Rancorous behavior and name-calling do not have the same normative appeal.

Even more recently, it is possible to tell stories of personality battles where the combatants are from the same political party. To cite an example of relationship conflict, in the twenty-first century, consider Senator Ted Cruz (R-TX), in 2015, accusing Majority Leader Mitch McConnell (R-KY) of being a "liar" on the Senate floor and repeating the affront multiple times in a raucous and mean-spirited fashion.[12] Traditional measures of partisan conflict would not capture this display of norm breaking or personalities, given that both senators represent the same political party.

In the 116th Congress (2019–2021), Speaker Nancy Pelosi (D-CA) was at odds with Alexandria Ocasio-Cortez (D-NY). The Representative from New York called for a change in leadership and faulted Democratic Party leaders for their failure to groom the next generation of Democratic lawmakers for leadership positions. A senior congressional Democrat commented, "Nancy doesn't have much patience for people who don't know what they don't know"[13] a direct reference to the speaker's feud with Ocasio-Cortez and other more progressive members of the Democratic Party caucus. In the 118th Congress (2023–25), it was Republican rank-and-file members Marjorie Taylor Greene (R-GA) and Lauren Boebert's (R-CO) turn to engage in intraparty relational conflict. Greene called Boebert "a little bitch" on the House floor.[14] The two far-right lawmakers were feuding over who would get credit for filing the necessary paperwork to initiate impeachment proceedings against President Joe Biden.

In each of the recent stories, the members engaging in relational conflict were from the same political party. Turns out, there are instances of intraparty personnel discord throughout the storied history of Congress. In chapter 2, we will learn that over 30 percent of all the incidents of relational conflict that I have chronicled for this book involve members of the same political party. One can imagine that this type of conflict may be useful in an era defined by elite collusion and avoidance of the important issues of the day. A rank-and-file member taking on party leaders might be required to break up the network of inter-party collusion and/or avoidance. Intraparty differences might create the necessary cleavages to structure meaningful policy debate. Yet, in an era defined by hyper-partisan conflict, seemingly, any additional conflict might be unhelpful. Especially, if the relational conflict is petty or lacks substance.

PARTISAN VERSUS RELATIONAL CONFLICT

LCT suggests that personality battles, like those just described, represent a second and unique dimension of legislative conflict. Moreover, I hold inter-party divergence over policy or affective polarization may exacerbate this second form of legislative conflict, but that inter-partisan differences alone are neither a necessary nor a sufficient condition to produce relational conflict or normlessness. Notably, many scholars who study conflict in the U.S. Congress are prone to only pay attention to partisan disagreement over policy, or more generally, party polarization measured by roll call voting behavior. I suggest these works, potentially, are missing something important about the totality of conflict in legislatures. This is especially important if uncivil discourse has unique effects on a competent legislative process, beyond that captured by differences in the voting behavior of members from the two major political parties. Ultimately, I will test this proposition.

My initial insights about two-dimensional legislative conflict were acquired in 1992, while surveying members of the House of Representatives who were leaving congressional service voluntarily at the end of the 102nd Congress. As I compiled responses from the early retirees, from both mail surveys and interviews, it became obvious that the members of this cohort of voluntary departures believed their jobs, of late, had become less attractive. Many of the respondents also made it clear what they believed to be important sources of the unpleasantness. Nearly all suggested either an increase in media attention to their personal lives or policy gridlock as part of their explanation for leaving the House. What is more telling are the attempts by former members to explain what they meant by making these specific claims. The retiring members tied the media scrutiny and gridlock considerations to some notion of a charged and increasingly uncivil congressional workplace. Furthermore, many of the respondents were convinced that their job had become more difficult and increasingly less meaningful because of the change.[15]

Theoretically, some amount of partisan policy disagreement and debate is essential to healthy legislative processes in a democracy. In a political system where elected members represent distinct constituencies, members disagreeing with one another at times seems sensible and even essential. Yet, it is *not* likely as important for members to disrespect the views of their political opponents. Nor are personal animosities and spiteful rhetoric obligatory. Indeed, a willingness to cooperate on a personal level with partisan opponents seems desirable and ought to aid effective lawmaking in an institution defined, in part, by checks and balances.

Scholars routinely attribute incivilities between members of Congress to high levels of party polarization (Loomis 2000; Sinclair 2000). This should not be surprising. It is quite easy to imagine the two types of conflict reinforcing one another. Disagreement over policy may be so intense that some members will express personal animosities toward each other. Alternatively, personal hostilities might cause members to disagree on policy for purely vindictive reasons. Yet, if partisan opponents ever get along, socially or personally, while maintaining their distinct policy preferences, this suggests two-dimensional conflict. Correspondingly, if there are people who hold very similar political views who cannot seem to get along, and dislike each other on a personal level, then, the two forms of conflict must be distinct. We can learn more about two-dimensional conflict by testing whether the people who are more prone to disagree on public policy are also more uncivil. Said differently, are the individuals who are responsible for high levels of party polarization in Congress, today, the same members most prone to act in an uncivil manner toward their workplace colleagues? This is an empirical question, which I will answer in chapter 3.

In studying two-dimensional legislative conflict, broadly, I treat Congress as a decision-making body, subject to the same types of workplace conflict that students of organizational behavior have found exist in private-sector settings (Pondy 1967). The first type of conflict these scholars identify is *"task conflict,"* which involves differences in viewpoints about how to best solve problems and promote an organization's mission (Shaw, Zhu, Duffy and Scott 2011). Task conflict, I hold, is analogous to the general partisan policy differences in legislatures often captured by summing up each party's roll call behavior and differencing the values. This is what many congressional scholars have done for some time now to capture conflict. The difference becomes the extent of party system polarization in a specific biennial Congress.

Business scholars often refer to the second type of organizational conflict as "relational conflict." Researchers define this type of conflict as workplace tension, annoyances, or personal incompatibility over values, habits, or personalities (De Dreu 2008, 6; *see also* Jehn 1995, 257–58). Relationship conflict is similar to the conflicts captured by the study of normlessness and incivility in Congress, which often results in the hurling of insults, name-calling, and even physical altercations.

To be clear, my concerns about incivility in the legislative process stem from the belief that unique opinions about alternative public policy options should be a healthy part of the democratic process. Legislators should express, and even argue passionately, alternative points of view in legislative settings. This is a fundamental aspect of effective discourse in a democracy. Name-calling, on the other hand, does not seem as important. Indeed, incivilities may poison the legislative environment in a manner that makes it more difficult to move legislation forward or otherwise get things done. Larry Dodd (1981) argued, a considerable time ago, that long-established norms of civility are what allow members of Congress to engage in meaningful debate while remaining within the bounds of courtesy and respect for their colleagues' perspectives. He notes that these discussions provide the best setting for the development of high-quality legislation. On the other hand, when courtesy norms are violated, sustained incivility can lead to a breakdown in personal relations, policymaking, and public trust in governing institutions (Cook and Gronke 2005).

There has been a well-documented increase in policy gridlock in Congress in modern times (Mayhew 1991; Binder 1999; 2017) and others find diminishing public support for Congress (Hibbing and Theiss-Morse 1995; Cooper 1999), and still others are concerned about the legislature's continuous submission to presidential authority (Jones 1994; Cooper 2017). The norm-centered perspective being espoused here suggests that much of the trends congressional scholars are uncovering may be attributable to a decline in civility in political discourse, which has occurred over the past thirty years (Uslaner 1993; Schraufnagel 2005; Dodd and Schraufnagel 2012). Some argue this recent pattern reflects contemporary social tensions (Uslaner 1993; 2000) and a reaction to the practice in the early years of the "Textbook Congress" of stifling congressional conflict (Burns 1963). Importantly, I suggest, the study of congressional incivility will shed considerable light and allow scholars to better understand the unique state of politics in the contemporary United States.

Others are less inclined to recognize incivility as an independent construct with unique implications for lawmaking. This interpretation uses a more structural or institutional-based explanation to understand conflict in Congress. According to this school of thought, the polarization of the two major political parties is what has caused the increase in incivility in Congress, as well as the rise in policy gridlock, the decline in public trust, and the increase in the power of the president (Cooper and Brady 1981; Rohde 1991; Bond and Fleisher 2000). Furthermore, proponents of this perspective argue that policy skirmishes breed policy gridlock, especially when smaller and/or less cohesive majority parties produce weak leaders. This may be especially relevant in the Senate where a small majority party will not be able to navigate the cloture rule, which requires a supermajority to pass legislation (Krehbiel 1993). In turn, partisan conflict causes the public to view Congress as slow moving and rarely capable of producing high-quality or important legislation, which in turn lowers support, and possibly trust in Congress (Hibbing and Theiss-Morse 1995).

Both the norm-centered perspective (see Alexander 2021) and the structural perspective suggest it is important to understand legislative conflict. What this book seeks to accomplish is to make it clear the two forms of conflict are distinct. Moreover, the intention is to promote a better understanding of an appropriate amalgam of the two types of conflict conducive to successful lawmaking. Consider Table 1.1, which submits theoretical expectations for the different mixtures of party polarization (task conflict) and incivilities (relational conflict). Note straightaway that the expectation is that too much conflict is problematic. However, too little conflict also presents a puzzle for effective lawmaking.

The expectation is that substantial and sustained productivity requires a Congress that fosters real policy contestation (Dahl 1967; 1971) characterized by some conflict, and perhaps even occasional incivilities, so that difficult policy problems are discussed and become salient (Jones and Baumgartner 2005; Schattschneider 1960). Such contestation limits the isolation of Congress and connects it with social reality. However, Congress then must maintain internal conflict within moderated parameters that avoid institutional meltdown, or government shutdowns, and enables deliberative policy making to proceed (Cooper 1970, Part IV; Maass 1983; Bessette 1994). In this formulation, too much institutional conflict can inhibit landmark productivity—but so can too little conflict.

I hold that too much conflict occurs in polarized Congresses, when high party polarization interacts with high inter-party or cross-party relational conflict. Many contemporary Congresses have experienced this harmful level of contestation and government shutdowns, and a seeming inability to address issues such as gun safety, immigration reform, and climate change have been commonplace. I hold one witness too little conflict in depolarized Congresses when low party polarization interacts with excessive inter-party niceties or intraparty differences. This low level of meaningful contestation can lead to cross-party collusion and avoidance as was witnessed in the mid-twentieth century when Southern Democrats and "lily white" Republicans[16] formed a conservative coalition capable of postponing legislative action on pressing civil rights concerns. In all of this, my contention will be that periods of congressional history characterized by a moderate level of interactive conflict between party polarization and member incivility will be the most productive.

Classic democratic theorist Robert Dahl (1967) makes it clear that severe conflict is problematic in a pluralistic republic. Yet, he continues, "to say that severe political conflict is undesirable is not to say that all political conflict is undesirable. So long as men have different views and the liberty to express their views, conflicts will exist. To condemn all political conflict as evil is to condemn diversity and liberty as evil" (1967, 270). Dahl's vision is reasonably clear; democracy should provide room for dissenting voices and that properly expressed, and effectively debated, these differences ought to aid competent lawmaking. Dahl also notes that moderate conflict is desirable and elaborates two means for attaining a median level of dispute in a republican system of

Table 1.1 Two-Dimensional Legislative Conflict and Legislative Productivity

		Party Polarization		
		High	Medium	Low
Relational Conflict	High	Gridlock	→	Productive
	Medium		Productive	
	Low	Productive	→	Gridlock

Source: Illustration by the author.

government. First, he recognizes the role played by political parties, which "help in the peaceful management of conflicts" (1967, 243). Specifically, he suggests partisan factions provide structure to competition among political leaders. Second, he recognizes the importance of parliamentary conventions and practices that enable legislatures "to negotiate internal conflicts peacefully" (Dahl 1967, 277). In this second instance, Dahl is suggesting that legislatures must have norms that encourage members to approach deliberation and negotiation in a spirit of mutual regard. Norms that cause partisan opponents to maintain civility in political discourse; lest conflict become too severe.

The specificity of Dahl's insights aside, what is lacking is a thorough elaboration of LCT. A theory that can withstand the test of time and be generalizable. I will provide overtime tests in this book; however, my hope is that follow-up scholarship will test the external validity of my thesis in different settings. In all this, it will be essential to define and operationalize parliamentary conflict carefully. Political scientists, studying the U.S. Congress, have routinely defined legislative discord in terms of political party polarization and captured the phenomenon using the distinctive voting behavior of partisan opponents (Roberts and Smith 2003; Poole and Rosenthal 2007; Garand 2010). I take no exception to this tactic and follow their lead. However, I suggest partisan roll call difference is only one dimension of conflict. Party polarization does not capture personnel attacks or heated rhetoric, fueled by mean-spiritedness or spite, another form of discord with the potential to derail efforts to address pressing societal problems, especially if party system polarization is already high.

Concepts such as two-dimensional legislative conflict, moderate conflict, and legislative productivity are broad in scope and quite difficult to operationalize. Yet, if the insights just shared have merit, it is imperative to move forward with these tasks. Chapter 2 tackles the measurement of the level of aggregate interactive conflict that has existed over a considerable swath of congressional history, while also systematically identifying individual legislators who have contributed to relational conflict. The thesis suggests that these individuals may aid productivity in certain historical periods while damaging legislative progress in other contexts. Chapter 3 will disentangle the two types of legislative conflict more completely and provide empirical evidence that proves the two phenomena are indeed distinct. Chapter 4 presents a study of the individual members of Congress who newspaper reports have implicated in incivilities. I will check into their backgrounds and look for systematic qualities that help to define the subset of legislators who have engaged in relational conflict. This can be helpful as we imagine the recruitment of quality legislators in the contemporary era.

Chapter 5 tackles the measurement of legislative productivity. In this instance, it will be necessary to capture "meaningful" legislative output while also considering the possibility that the demand for legislative action is dynamic. Chapter 6 is where the rubber will meet the road. I will provide a series of tests of the relationship between two-dimensional moderate conflict and legislative productivity. Being careful to distinguish intraparty and interparty relational conflict and offering unique tests of their dissimilar effects on legislative competence, overtime. Chapter 7 will offer policy prescriptions for managing conflict as we move through the twenty-first century Congresses. This final chapter will also provide a final test of the precepts of LCT using case studies of uncivil members in four different historical periods.

NOTES

1. My contention is that these two dimensions of conflict exist in all social circles including family, private-sector workplaces, and neighborhoods. However, it is their manifestation in the public sector, which is of particular consequence, as it relates to the good of society and hence, it is conflict in Congress, which will be the focus of this work.
2. Editorial, *New York Times*, September 4, 1890, 1.
3. Editorial, *New York Times*, September 4, 1890, 1.
4. Editorial, *New York Times*, September 4, 1890, 1.
5. Editorial, *Washington Post*, February 23, 1902, 1.
6. Editorial, *Washington Post*, February 23, 1902, 1.
7. Editorial, *Washington Post* February 23, 1902, 1.
8. Editorial, *Washington Post*, February 23, 1902, 1.
9. For a description of one of the most famous, and gruesome, instances of violence in Congress, see Hull Hoffer and William James (2010). The book tells the story of the caning of Charles Sumner (R-MA) by Preston Brooks (D-SC).
10. Lois Romano. "Dual on the Hill." *Washington Post*, March 6, 1985, C1.
11. Irvin Molotsky. "A Senator is captured, but Not His Mind." *New York Times*, February 25, 1988, A-26.
12. Manu Raju. 2015. "Cruz accuses Mitch McConnell of telling a 'flat-out lie'." *Politico*, https://www.politico.com/story/2015/07/ted-cruz-says-mitch-mcconnell-lies-export-import-bank-120583 (last accessed March 12, 2022).
13. Susan Page. 2021. "Inside Nancy Pelosi's War with AOC and the Squad." *Politico*, April 15, https://www.politico.com/news/magazine/2021/04/15/nancy-pelosi-alexandria-ocasio-cortez-481704 (last accessed September 12, 2023).
14. Victor Nava. 2023. "Rep. Marjorie Taylor Greene calls fellow Republican Lauren Boebert a "little bitch" during heated argument on House floor: report." *New York Post*, https://nypost.com/2023/06/21/marjorie-taylor-greene-calls-lauren-boebert-little-bitch-on-house-floor/ (last accessed September 12, 2023).
15. There has been considerable research done on the large class of retirees from the 102nd Congress. Many have found that issues involving the House Bank and a change in House Rules that allowed members of the House a last opportunity to convert excess campaign funds to personal use were responsible for the large number

of voluntary departures that year (see Groseclose and Krehbiel 1994; Jacobson and Dimock 1994). I suspect these findings are accurate. Indeed, many of the respondents to my mail survey and in the interviews indicated these were controlling factors. Nonetheless, I believe that my conclusion that a changed and charged legislative environment motivated many members to retire is also part of the explanation.

16. A lily-white Republican is a historical reference to a faction within the Republican Party who were opposed to the political and socioeconomic gains made by African Americans following the Civil War (https://www.tshaonline.org/handbook/entries/lily-white-movement, last accessed December 20, 2022).

Chapter 2

Measuring Conflict in Legislatures

In chapter 1, I made the case for two-dimensional conflict in legislatures. Organizational scholars studying private-sector productivity see two-dimensional conflict occurring in all workplaces. I concur. However, the focus here is squarely on the U.S. Congress. In previous work, I was able to use survey data to measure the level of policy disagreement versus relational conflict in Illinois local legislatures (Yuan and Schraufnagel 2019). The research found that city officials who reported more relational conflict also perceived the local legislatures as less effective. Importantly, when this same group of respondents reported more policy differences on the local Council, the perception was associated with a positive view of Council effectiveness. The findings suggest there is value to differences in opinion regarding public policy, but that relational conflict does not add anything. It is my hope that anyone interested in competent legislatures, anywhere in the world, will consider the precepts of Legislative Conflict Theory (LCT), especially the value of moderation, as they wrestle with appropriate rules for debate and quality institutional arrangements but also legislator recruitment.

To produce tests of the value of moderate conflict in legislatures, it is necessary to develop appropriate measurement strategies. In the social sciences, and perhaps all sciences, measurement is always a thorny issue. If there were a perfectly valid manner for capturing any phenomenon of interest, one would not need to develop a measure of the concept. Relational conflict born of normlessness, spite, or a lack of civility is a particularly difficult concept to grapple with and operationalize. Exacerbating the trouble in this case is the need for a longitudinal indicator capable of capturing the dynamic nature of each dimension of legislative conflict. Specifically, I wish to show that the two dimensions of conflict have existed in Congress, at varying levels, over a considerable period. I suspect that sometimes the two modes of conflict will reinforce one another, while at other times diverge. To do this, I need measurement strategies with values over many Congresses. Thankfully, efforts to measure party polarization, or partisan policy divergence, are quite mature. Scholars have been fine-tuning measurement strategies for this dimension of legislative conflict for over 100 years. I will review those efforts and settle on a suitable measure quite easily. I begin, however, with the much more unique measurement of relational conflict, which results in the breaking of civility norms based on courtesy and mutual respect.[1]

MEASURING RELATIONAL CONFLICT

To determine the presence of relational conflict in our personal lives is quite simple. Does so-and-so make you mad? Does their behavior or perhaps their very existence upset you? To measure relational conflict in an organization is much less straightforward. Surveys of members of Congress might work if they existed going back into the nineteenth century, but that is not the case. Left with limited options, I draw on contemporaneous newspaper reporting to identify instances when members have been at odds with one another. The use of media reports most certainly underestimates the level of relational conflict in a particular Congress. The animosities must be sufficiently grievous to cause public displays of anger that capture the attention of newspaper reporters. Yet, I have no reason to believe that the underrepresentation of personality battles, or relational conflict, is higher in a particular era of congressional history.

When studying Congress, the use of media reporting, as a measurement strategy, is not unique. My use of newspaper articles follows the lead of David Mayhew (1991) and Sarah Binder (1999), both of whom examine *New York Times* coverage of Congress to assess legislative productivity in the post–World War II era. Moreover, my effort to delineate historical patterns in congressional behavior through the coding of member activity as reported in published documents, in my case the *New York Times* (*Times*) and *Washington Post* (*Post*), parallels David Mayhew's efforts (2000) to code member activity as reported in major texts of American history. In another instance, Jeffery Mondak (1995) measures legislator competence by systematic study of biographies provided by the *Almanac of American Politics*.

Specifically, I will gauge the level of relational conflict, Congress by Congress, according to the number of articles printed in the *Times* and the *Post* that discuss incidents of members of Congress not getting along with one another. I will be especially keen to find articles that discuss the breaking of civility norms, which emphasize decorum and mannerly policy deliberation. I assume in doing so that a larger number of articles devoted to norm breaking incivilities indicates greater levels of relational conflict in Congress.[2] The two newspapers I use have been in continuous publication for a considerable length of time, which provides the extended timeline necessary to test the merits of Legislative Conflict Theory (LCT). I have searched the *Times* going back to 1851 and the *Post* going back to 1877. Because in the end I use a two-newspaper average, I begin the measurement of relational conflict with the 45th Congress (1877–1879).

I chose to use the *Times* because many considered it the "newspaper of record" for national affairs in the United States (Martin and Hansen 1998). Correspondingly, I expect the *Times* would report on serious acts of incivility in Congress, relevant to national politics and governance. I chose the *Post* because it is the longest continuously published major newspaper in the nation's capital focused on the workings of Congress. I would expect the *Post* to be alert, on a daily basis, to serious incidents of personalities happening on Capitol Hill. Combining the newspapers provides a systematic, and replicable, way to capture the range and national importance of incidents of relational conflict, over a considerable period. I encourage others to use similar strategies via content analysis of different periodicals or other continuously available forms of media. My count of acts of relational conflict, Congress by Congress, can serve as a baseline for comparison and assessment of the results of other strategies.

To search the newspapers, I rely on the search engine provided by *Pro-Quest*, which has historical online archives for both newspapers. The initial search used the terms "Congress," "House of Representatives," and "Senate" in the full text with any of the following terms: "rancor," "comity," "civility," "incivility," "courteous," "courtesy," "discourteous," "discourtesy," "trust and anger," "discord," and "collegiality"; also, in the full text. A second search specifies that "Congress," "House," or "Senate" has to appear in the title with any of the following terms in the full text: "personalities," "grudge," "raucous," "insolence," "contempt," "amity," "lack of good will," "impertinence," "brash," "audacious," "hot-headed," "heated," "disrespect," "lack of respect," and "discordant."

The combined search nets over 15,000 articles during the years studied, from the two newspapers combined. I can dismiss many articles by reading the headline or the first few sentences of the article. Common misses included articles on the African National Congress and the New York, Virginia, and Maryland state legislatures. I needed to read many other articles more carefully to determine if the discussion was relevant to the contemporaneous Congress. The articles included specific instances of norm-breaking incivilities or personal conflict between legislators when these result in mean-spirited sarcasm or snide remarks, the hurling of insults, name-calling, finger-wagging, red faces, and physical altercations. I use only articles that call attention to these behaviors when the legislators are acting in their official capacity as members of the current Congress. I do not count stories about incivilities by members when they served in an earlier Congress, incivilities that occur while they are visiting their districts, or incivilities directed at an opponent in the context of an election campaign. Ultimately, the process nets 957 *New York Times* articles and 962 *Washington Post* articles from 1877 to 2021.[3]

Figure 2.1 presents the count of articles on incivility as reported in the *Times* and *Post* by Congress from the 45th (1877–1879) to the 116th (2019–2021). As this figure makes clear, Congress is not a Sunday school picnic and there has been considerable jousting among members for the 144 years studied. Indeed, all seventy-two Congresses experienced relational conflict that gained the notice of newspaper reporters and forty-seven of the seventy-two Congresses studied had a double-digit number of articles in both newspapers. In the twenty-first century, all Congresses except the 107th (2001–2003), which was serving during the terrorist attacks that occurred on September 11, 2001, experienced more than ten articles in both newspapers. The dip in displays of member animosities, during the 107th Congress, while the nation attempted to make sense of the terrorist attacks, is precisely what one would expect. Given the solemnity of the times, it makes sense that members would be less inclined to berate one another publically. At least temporarily.

Quite notably, values from the two newspapers are highly correlated in a statistically significant manner over the seventy-two observations ($r = .68$, $P < .001$). The correlation creates a sort of mutual validation of the measurement strategy. Indeed, reporters from both major newspapers often cover many of the same instances of personal battles. My intention was always to combine the two newspaper values, because as noted, I believe each newspaper brings something unique to the table. The *Times'* coverage, in effect, is a check on the seriousness or gravity of the incident and the *Post* ought to improve the breadth of coverage given it is "on the ground" in the nation's capital. Differences aside, the high bivariate correlation between coverage in the *Times* and *Post* lends a form of credibility to my decision to combine the two newspaper values.

It is quite easy to see the strong relationship between the two newspaper values in figure 2.1. For instance, notice corresponding peaks and valleys representing coverage of personality battles in the two newspapers. Although there are certainly some incongruences, there is considerable symmetry. For instance, based on reporting in both newspapers, there is a dip in relational outbursts in the 58th Congress (1903–1905), the first full Congress after the assassination of President William McKinley. There is also less relational conflict reported in both newspapers during World War II. Next, notice the corresponding valleys in the first half of the 1970s when members collectively were dealing with considerable public disapproval

Measuring Conflict in Legislatures 23

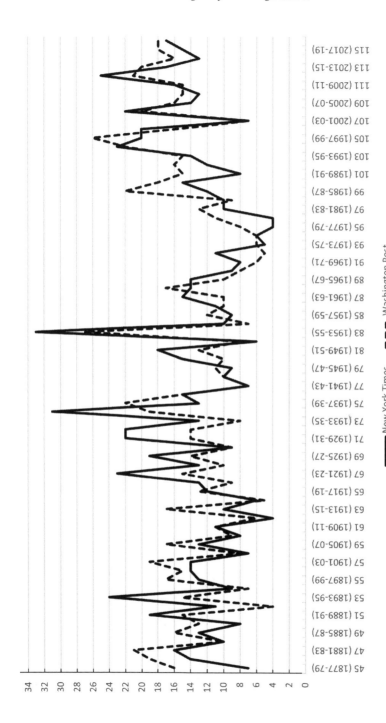

Figure 2.1 The Count of the Number of Articles in the *New York Times* and *Washington Post* by Congress. *Source:* Compiled by the author.

of the prolonged Vietnam War, while the Watergate scandal was causing dismay and consternation among elites and the public alike. I have already noted the drop in both newspapers during the 107th Congress. I wish to make perfectly clear that the dip in the 107th occurs in a period of intense two-party polarization. The terrorist's strikes of 9/11, followed by the war in Afghanistan, seemed to have a sobering effect, albeit brief. The nation and members of Congress rallied in a unified manner, with members presumably avoiding high interpersonal conflict despite the broader polarization of the era defined by distinct major party voting behavior. In turn, Congress was able to pass the USA Patriot Act (P.L. 107–56) and the Aviation and Transportation Act (P.L. 107–71), which created the Transportation Security Administration.

More generally, the relational conflict values, based on newspaper reports, make some intuitive sense. For instance, values are low in the mid-twentieth century, when the conservative coalition and committee government dominated Congress and classic literature on Congress suggests that apprenticeship and civility norms were quite strong (Matthews 1959). Yet, substantial moments of incivility did occur midcentury at points that make sense, despite the existence of committee government and the conservative coalition. Note the spikes in the 74th (1935–1936) and 83rd (1953–1955) Congresses when newspapers were covering the antics of Huey Long (D-LA), Joseph McCarthy (R-WI), and their detractors. The boisterous and flamboyant character of Huey Long (D-LA) during the mid-Great Depression, is legendary (Sindler 1956). In the 83rd Congress, McCarthy was always ratchetting up the level of discourteous outbursts and reporters at both newspapers reported on this. In all, the 74th and 83rd Congress peaks make sense.

Particularly intriguing about the 74th Congress, dominated by the conduct of Senator Long, is that of the thirty-one articles in the *Times*, only four represent inter-party conflict. In the *Post*, only five of nineteen were inter-party. I code the other articles as either intraparty or nonpartisan. Intraparty relational conflict occurs when the combatants are from the same political party. I code articles "nonpartisan," if the story is about a single member's character and antics, without drawing attention to another member of Congress or some other partisan government official. In the 74th, many articles covered the Democratic senator from Louisiana delivering scathing denunciations of his copartisan, President Franklin D. Roosevelt, from the Senate floor. In others, he was at odds with his Senate Majority Leader Joseph T. Robinson (D-AR). The *Times* reported that Senator Long, speaking to Robinson and wagging his finger in his face, stated, "There'll be no hand shaking this time." Long's outburst was a reaction to a speech made by Robinson about the newly created Civilian Conservation Corps. The majority leader stated:

> When the senator from Louisiana ridicules the President's efforts to redeem and safe this asset of incalculable—value and what can be of more value, than the young, the enlightened manhood of the United States—I ask him: Has he no sense of responsibility when he speaks? Month after month, the senator from Louisiana has disgusted this body with repeated attacks on men who are superior to him, with repeated efforts to discredit the President and to humiliate him.[4]

In one of the articles coded as "nonpartisan" a *Times* editorial comments on the mischiefs of Senator Long, reporting: "Not for many years has the urbanity of the Senate been so completely shattered as during the debates which have centered about the picturesque personality and equally picturesque proposals of Huey Long."[5] Although the "debates" mentioned were primarily intraparty, because the article does not cite specific instances of copartisan infighting, I code it as "nonpartisan."

In the 83rd Congress, of the thirty-three articles found in *Times* reporting, thirty of them are about personal battles in the Senate where the Army-McCarthy hearings were taking place throughout 1953 and early 1954. Correspondingly, twenty-five out of the twenty-seven *Post* articles covered relational incivilities in the Upper Chamber. During the hearings, McCarthy alleged Communist influence in the press and the federal government, including the State Department, the U.S. Army, and the Government Printing Office. What some fail to appreciate is that McCarthy was a particularly caustic individual and had no difficulty fomenting relational conflict throughout his time in the Senate. This was particularly evident during proceedings related to his ultimate censure in December of 1954. A favorite McCarthy tactic was to chide other members in a manner that would cause them to react. A staff writer for the *Post* notes, "Senator Joseph R. McCarthy yesterday gave testimony in sweeping contradiction to sworn charges against himself and his staff, in a hearing which ended with his own counsel and the Democrats' attorney close to fisticuffs."[6]

It is important to note, I use total newspaper *articles* to gauge the level of relational conflict rather than determining the precise number of acts of incivility that occur in a given Congress. Hence, included in the database are multiple articles that focus on a single incident. My assumption is that especially serious acts of uncivil relations will generate multiple news stories. This, in effect, creates a weighting element to the analysis that serves to provide a comparative estimate of the level of serious incivility that is occurring in each Congress. I do not give numerical weight to acts of incivility according to my own judgment of the severity of the incident. Last, it needs mentioning that I pulled the names of individual members of Congress from these articles to use in a couple of different ways. I will use the individual's mentioned as engaging in relational conflict in chapter 3 when testing for difference between ideologically extreme members and uncivil members. My suspicion is that they are not the same and that one can be a partisan, even ideologically extreme, while maintaining good personal relationships with other members. I will also briefly use these individuals in chapter 7 when testing the legislative effectiveness of uncivil members of Congress in different periods of congressional history. Here, my suspicion is that uncivil members might be more effective when party system polarization is low and less effective when it is high.[7]

Finally, as indicated in chapter 1, during the conceptual discussion of legislative conflict, it is important to distinguish between inter-party and intraparty relational conflict. The information about partisan context will help make clear the nature of two-dimensional legislative conflict, which is occurring in different historical periods. Theoretically, different types of conflicts can have quite distinct effects on legislative effectiveness, under different polarization scenarios. For instance, high inter-party relational conflict in an era of high party system polarization, I suggest, is a prescription for legislative gridlock. Especially, given the super majoritarian requirements found in the U.S. legislative process. Sufficient intraparty incivilities, on the other hand, may cause crosscutting partisan cleavages capable of producing majority support for a particular policy proposal. Nonpartisan norm breaking, by a single individual, without an obvious target for their animosity, might also be valuable at certain times. Perhaps the antagonism of a single member will cause competing partisans to cooperate with one another, even if only temporarily, to take a principled stand against the norm-breaking incivilities of the belligerent one.

In some of the policy productivity testing, found in chapter 6, I will focus on inter-party relational conflict and leave intraparty and nonpartisan incivilities as omitted categories. I consider both theoretically distinct from inter-party mischief or inter-party relational difficulties. Considering the partisan context of the relational conflict found in the two newspapers, I determine that 502 *Times* articles (52.5 percent) and 496 *Post* articles (51.6 percent) dealt with debate that led to obvious relational conflict between individuals from different political parties. I also find 294 *Times* articles (30.7 percent) and 301 *Post* articles (31.4 percent) discussing animosities or norm-breaking incivilities involving members of the same political party. Lastly, 161 *Times* articles and 164 *Post* articles report on the hostility of a single member or, less commonly, made mention of relational conflict in Congress as a whole, without indicating a partisan context.

Figure 2.2 presents the variation in inter-party versus intraparty incivilities, by Congress, from the 45th to the 116th, and makes it clear that these are quite distinct aspects of relational conflict. Note, at the beginning and the end of the time series that inter-party relational conflict nearly always surpasses intraparty conflict. An exception is the 114th Congress where intraparty relational

Measuring Conflict in Legislatures 27

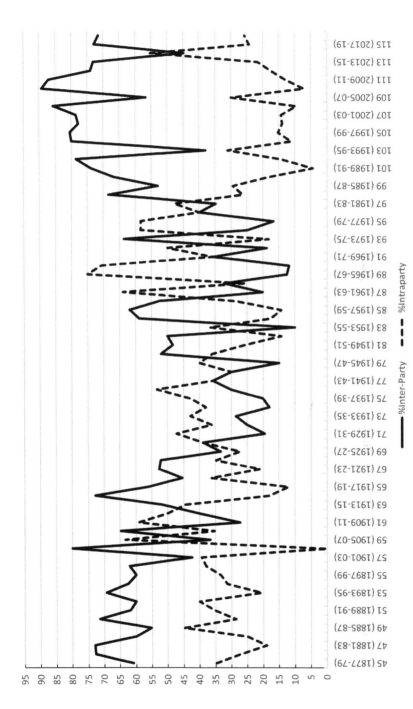

Figure 2.2 The Percentage of Articles in the *New York Times* and *Washington Post* (combined) by Congress that deal with Inter- vs. Intraparty Relational Conflict. *Source:* Compiled by the author.

conflict reaches 55 percent. This is the Congress when Ted Cruz (R-TX) not only calls his party leader Mitch McConnell (R-KY) a liar repeatedly, but also the Congress that witnessed considerable intraparty battles between members of the Republican House Freedom Caucus and their speaker, John Boehner (R-OH). Both newspapers mention each of these instances of intraparty name-calling and caustic behavior in more than one article.

Notably, the broader trend of high inter-party relational conflict at both the beginning and the end of the time series is in keeping with what we know about party polarization or the distinctive voting behavior of Democrats and Republicans. Party polarization was higher at the end of the nineteenth century and the beginning of the twenty-first century and inter-party relational conflict follows this pattern. This finding suggests that the two types of conflict can be mutually reinforcing. Yet, for 70+ years from the early 1900s into the 1970s, it is much more of a mixed bag. Notably, during this period, it is quite common for intraparty incivilities to outpace inter-party relational conflict. The increased intraparty incivility of the 1960s and 1970s fits with the sense that the great changes occurring in Congress were intraparty in character more than inter-party. The resolution of the intraparty fights, particularly within the majority Democratic Party, came through the adoption of various reforms in rules and procedures and through the Southern realignment. These changes brought the disappearance of "old school" Southern conservative Democrats and the rise of a Southern conservative Republican Party, setting the stage for the rise of high inter-party conflict thereafter. The increase in intraparty incivilities also parallels the emergence of policy productivity during and after the New Frontier and Great Society Congresses.

Overall, I believe my effort to measure variation in incivility within Congress across a considerable swath of time yields patterns that have reasonable face validity. Importantly, I have archived all the articles used to produce these values, and these are available to the public. Often, while writing this book, I learned Congress-specific values of inter-party or intraparty relational conflict that initially surprised me. For instance, the high level of intraparty battles in the 114th Congress. Yet, when referring to the archives, I learn straightway what specific battles were occurring that produced the values, and the coding makes sense anew. Next up, it is necessary to settle on an appropriate measure of party polarization that spans the seventy-two Congresses I am studying.

MEASURING PARTY POLARIZATION

As noted earlier, scholars have been studying party difference for a considerable period, and there are many alternative ways to measure the "polarization" of the two major political parties in the U.S. Congress. For instance, Lawrence Lowell (1902), over a century ago, developed "party votes" or the percentage of times that a majority of Democrats vote in opposition to a majority of Republicans. Not long after that, Stuart Rice (1928) developed the "Rice Index" of intraparty cohesion. Then in 1970, Julius Turner and Edward Schneier (1970) published their work on "party unity" values, and Duncan MacRae (1970) published his "percent agreement" scores. More recently, John Coleman (1997) developed a "dissimilarity" measure, calculated by taking the absolute value of the difference between the proportion of Democrats and the proportion of Republicans who voted yes on a set of roll call votes. Still, others have used party platforms or manifestos to establish partisan difference (Ginsberg 1972; Budge, Klingemann, and Tanenbaum 2001), while others have attempted to use elite surveys to distinguish the parties. For instance, in 1999 two book chapters were published that surveyed delegates to either national or state party conventions (*see* Green, Jackson, and Clayton 1999; Stone, Rapoport, and Abramowitz 1999).

We can find still more scholars grappling with party polarization who use the *National Election Study*, a survey produced by the University of Michigan. These scholars analyze responses from the subset of participants who hold political jobs (Holsti and Rosenau 1996). Still others make use of a CBS/*New York Times* survey of congressional candidates during the 1982 election cycle (Wright and Berkman 1986) to distinguish the policy preferences of the two major political parties. Next, scholars have used interest group ratings such as those produced by the *Americans for Democratic Action* (ADA) to measure the polarization of the two major political parties (Lebo, McGlynn, and Koger 2007; Shapiro 2011). Last, some distinguish the ideological or policy preferences of the political parties using *Project Vote Smart's* biennial survey of congressional candidates called the Congressional National Political Awareness Test (Schraufnagel and Mondak 2002). What is striking about all alternative measures of party polarization is the high level of over time correlation between them all.[8]

Table 2.1 displays the inter-item correlation of seven of the different measures just mentioned. One must anticipate the negative bivariate correlations for the "Percent Agreement" (MacRae 1970) indicator because the measure is tapping two-party cooperation and not party polarization. The strong correlations are expected; scholars have long claimed, "The song stays the same" and there are just not stark differences between the alternative measures of polarization" (Burden, Caldeira, and Groseclose 2000, 237). This is not to suggest that a particular measure is never preferable. Conceivably, survey data, roll call votes, or party platform data are more appropriate depending on the specific research question(s) scholars are trying to answer. In my case,

Table 2.1 Measuring Party Polarization in the House of Representatives: 1933-2000

	Party Votes	Party Unity Scores	Unlikeness	Rice Index	Percent Agreement	ADA [a]	DW-Nominate
Party Votes	1	.69**	.88**	.63**	-.65**	.79**	.87**
		(68)	(68)	(68)	(68)	(46)	(46)
Party Unity Scores		1	.89**	.29*	-.82**	.59**	.53**
			(68)	(68)	(68)	(46)	(46)
Unlikeness			1	.49**	-.82**	.59**	.74**
				(68)	(68)	(46)	(46)
Rice Index				1	.04	.87**	.82**
					(68)	(46)	(46)
Percent Agreement					1	-.25	-.30*
						(46)	(46)
ADA						1	.94**
							(46)
DW-Nominate							1

I am constrained by the need for data that covers 144 years of congressional history.

In the end, I adopt the use of the DW-NOMINATE scores developed by Keith Poole and Howard Rosenthal (1997). These scores are arguably the most routinely used measure of two-party ideological or roll call difference (e.g., Hixon and Wicks 2000; Binder and Maltzman 2002) and the data is readily available for the entire history of Congress. In addition, as one can see in table 2.1, these scores correlate with the alternative measures at a high rate, always in the expected direction, and in a statistically significant manner. Relying on these scores, I measure party polarization by calculating the absolute value of the difference between the first and second largest parties' median first dimension DW-NOMINATE score. There is a separate calculation for each chamber and for each Congress from the 45th to the 116th.

Figure 2.3 displays chamber-specific values for each Congress. Note the very high correlation between House and Senate values ($r = .902$; $P < .00$; $n = 72$). Looking at party polarization, one notes that it has varied greatly across time and in a waved or even cyclical manner rather than the sporadic manner of relational conflict (see Figure 2.1). Party polarization was high in the late nineteenth and early twentieth centuries. It then began declining roughly midway through the Howard Taft Administration and fell below the average polarization score in the Herbert Hoover Administration. Thereafter, it declined to a highly *de*polarized status from the New Deal years through the early post-war Congresses. The level of partisan difference on roll call votes climbed into a more moderately depolarized status during the presidency of John F. Kennedy and through the Jimmy Carter Administration. Once we reach the 1980s, the trend is clearly established, and we move into the highly polarized Congresses of the twenty-first century.

The dip in polarization in the 47th Senate (1881–1883) warrants mentioning. The Upper Chamber had thirty-seven Democrats, thirty-seven Republicans, and two-independents. One of the independents, David Davis (I-IL), voted with the Democrats. The other, William Mahone (I-VA), voted with Republicans, however, only after extracting considerable concessions.[9] This gave Republicans majority control with Vice President Chester A. Arthur (R-NY) casting tie-breaking votes. That is until Arthur became president on September 19, 1881, with the death of President James A. Garfield, who died of wounds from an assassin's bullet. After assuming the presidency, Arthur called the Senate into an extraordinary session.

The highly polarized Senate took a turn toward moderation and there was considerable bipartisan compromise for the remainder of the 47th Congress. This explains the dip in the polarization value seen in figure 2.3. One can also recognize the solemnity of the times, in the aftermath of a presidential assassination, with the dip in relational conflict that occurs in the 48th Congress.

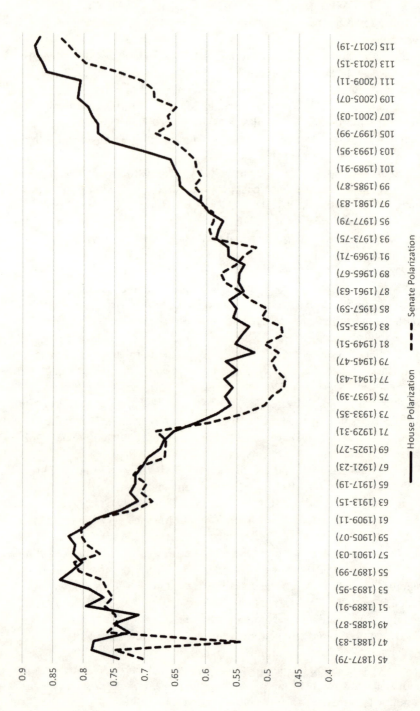

Figure 2.3 The Difference between Democrat and Republican Chamber Median DW-NOMINATE Scores (House and Senate). *Source:* voteview.com, https://voteview.com/data

A reduction in aggregate relational conflict in the 47th Congress was not possible because of the antics of Senator Roscoe Conkling (R-NY) who resigned mid-term over a personal battle with Senator Thomas Platt (R-NY). Another same-state intraparty relational battle. Notably, newspaper reports mentioned Conkling in fourteen different articles during his time in Congress, four times in the 47th Congress.

Ultimately, in the testing that follows, I opt to use the measure of Senate polarization. Given bicameralism and the need to pass legislation in both chambers, party discipline ought to matter in both chambers, and one might consider a two-chamber average polarization score. However, Poole and Rosenthal (1997) warn against averaging chamber values. The scholars note that they are not considering the same set of votes or policies when constructing the chamber-specific scores. I suggest that Senate polarization is more relevant because of the extra obstructionist opportunity provided by the filibuster in the Upper Chamber.[10]

MEASURING MODERATE LEGISLATIVE CONFLICT

The theory espoused by Robert Dahl (1967; 1971) argues that moderate legislative conflict is most desirable. He is particularly concerned with avoiding hyper-conflict, while recognizing that some conflict is inherent in a democratically elected legislature. Building on his work, I hold that the salient type of member conflict, and the relationship between legislative conflict and policy productivity, ought to differ in depolarized and polarized Congresses. For depolarized Congresses, I hold, *intraparty* incivility is the more salient dimension of member conflict. The mid-twentieth century, which witnessed a conservative coalition of Southern Democrats and Republicans voting together to prevent progressive reforms. This era is arguably too depolarized and there is not sufficient legislative conflict to prompt action. Under depolarization, one might imagine that intraparty relational conflict might rock the boat of inter-party collusion and prompt policy movement. Conversely, when Congress is highly polarized, as it has been throughout the first decades of the twenty-first century, seemingly any type of relational conflict will produce the hyper-conflict that Dahl imagines problematic. Inter-party incivilities ought to be particularly harmful to productivity.

To initiate an empirical assessment of these arguments, it is again necessary to develop a measurement strategy. I begin by developing an indicator of moderate-party system polarization. I do this by folding the Senate party polarization data displayed in figure 2.3. Precisely, I order the Congresses from the most depolarized to the most polarized and calculate the median value, which is .66077. All Congresses with a polarization value lower than the median simply maintain their value. In these depolarized settings, as values increase, one moves toward more moderation. Then, one must consider the Congresses above the median polarization value. In these cases, the values must be "folded."

Specifically, I subtract the previous polarization value from the value I wish to convert. I then use this difference to subtract it from the previous value, which converts that value, and all subsequent values above the median, to smaller numbers preserving the relevant distance between values. To illustrate, if you have five observations, .15, .18, .26, .34, and .45. For the values leading up to the median, including the median, I just keep the values the same (.15, .18, and .26). I need to maintain the median value as the largest number. To obtain the fourth value, it is necessary to subtract the previous value from the fourth value (.34 − .26 = .08). Then subtract this difference from the previous value (.26 − .08 = .18). The new fourth value now equals .18. One must do this for all the values greater than the median value. To finish, (.45 − .34 = .11), then (.18 − .11 = .07). The fifth value now equals .07. Ordering the moderation values, I get .26, .18, .18, .15, and .07. Note, the median value is the highest, and in this example, the values that had been on each side of the median are now both .18. This is because the previous values were equidistant from the median. The previous extreme high value of .45 is now the lowest value .07.

I present the folded data, or moderation values, in figure 2.4. Notice there is one line for the entire time-series and a second line for the 67th (1921–1923) Congress to the 116th Congress (2019–2021). In chapter 4, I will introduce a new measure of "Topical Legislative Productivity" and that data is available only from 1921 forward. Because I will run tests of the moderation thesis using this more abbreviated period, I present this moderation data in the figure 2.4 as well. When determining whether a Congress is moderate, I suggest, it is relevant to compare it to the other Congresses being considered. Hence, the two timelines.

Note first, in figure 2.3, when considering the abbreviated timeline, the level of moderation falls off more quickly in the contemporary era. Once I no longer consider the late nineteenth century Congresses, the current era looks even more immoderate. I find the late nineteenth-century Congresses highly polarized (see Figure 2.3) and in many respects on par with levels of polarization witnessed in much of the early years of the twenty-first century. Throughout the mid-twentieth century, the calculation of moderate party system polarization produces identical values considering both timelines. The relative level of moderation is the same and quite low. Now, the problem is not severe conflict, but too little conflict. The political parties are not disciplined or responsible and this causes consternation for the American Political Science Association (APSA), which calls for the two major political parties

Measuring Conflict in Legislatures

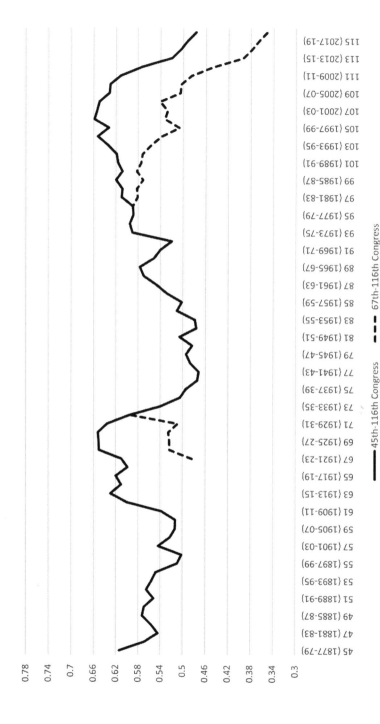

Figure 2.4 **Moderate Party Polarization.** *Source*: Compiled by the author from data available at voteview.com, voteview.com/data.

to distinguish themselves and to discipline their member's voting behavior (APSA 1950; see also Schattschneider 1960).

David Rohde (1991) notes that the logic of politics in the House of Representatives shifted subtly but rapidly during the 1980s—though the foundations for the shift had emerged in incremental ways over the previous several decades. The easiest way to think of the shift, in Rohde's terms, is that it involved a move from the textbook-era of Congress, characterized by depolarized politics and committee government, to a period of conditional party government characterized by an increase in the power of leaders and consequent party polarization. Accordingly, the mid-twentieth century is considered insufficiently polarized, the political parties are too undisciplined, leaders lack procedural power, and considering LCT there is not sufficient conflict to produce meaningful landmark legislative achievements.

Looking at the entire time series, and the solid line, the median moderation value is .569. Congresses falling below the line marked 0.54, in the figure 2.4 are less moderate, on average, and those Congresses above the 0.58 line are more moderate on average. Toward the end of the time-series, note the first Congress of President Barack Obama, the 111th (2009–11), is still above the median value before things fall off precipitously. The 111th Congress produced the American Recovery and Reinvestment Act, the Lily Ledbetter Fair Pay Act, and the Affordable Care Act (Obamacare) among other notable legislative achievements. The mid-1960s Congresses, with President Lyndon Johnson's notable legislative accomplishments (food stamps, Medicare, and Medicaid) also occur when moderation was at or above the median level. Last, as noted previously, the 1940s and 1950s when the conservative coalition was most powerful are more immoderate or insufficiently polarized. The era witnesses considerable across-party collusion and avoidance on the issues of civil rights, the environment, and urban blight. In theory, there was not sufficient party discipline to structure meaningful policy debate and prompt policy action.

There is another way to test the moderation thesis. Some might imagine an interaction between party polarization and relational conflict. The two types of conflict at high levels, working in tandem, may have especially adverse effects on legislative productivity. When party polarization is high, inter-party relational conflict ought to be especially problematic. Intraparty and nonparty relational conflict, on the other hand, may help. Put differently, too much two-dimensional inter-party conflict ought to inhibit legislative productivity—but when party polarization is high, intraparty and nonpartisan relational conflict might cause a thaw in hyper-conflict sufficient to witness some cross-party communication and compromise.

To cite a real-world example of what I am suggesting, consider the 118th Congress (2021–23). In theory, intraparty wrangling among Republicans who support former President Donald Trump and their co-partisans who are less enamored by the former chief executive may cause an intraparty rift. The dissension in their ranks may cause the majority Republicans, in the House of Representatives, to be a less potent obstacle to the legislative initiatives of the Joseph Biden Administration. Yet, it is also likely that extreme party polarization in the 118th Congress means any uptick of relational conflict, of any character, will move the country into the "severe" conflict arena that Dahl (1967) saw as problematic for pluralist democracies.

To summarize, I argue that too much conflict occurs in polarized Congresses, those above the historic median level, when there is high party polarization and high inter-party or cross-party relational incivilities. On the other hand, too little conflict occurs in depolarized Congresses, especially when there is low party polarization and inter-party comradery (or intraparty relational conflict). In other words, the interactive conflict between party polarization and relational conflict may foster landmark productivity in both depolarized and polarized Congresses, depending on the partisan context of relational conflict. Put as succinctly as possible, high polarization and inter-party relational conflict ought to associate with less productivity, high polarization and intraparty relational conflict ought to associate with an improved chance of legislative accomplishment. In the end, it is important to consider that all conflict is not the same nor is all conflict necessarily bad. In a democratically elected legislature, the proper management of conflict is the paramount consideration.

Figure 2.5 displays the values on the interaction term just discussed. Specifically, the interaction is Senate party polarization, based on aggregate DW-NOMINATE first dimension party difference, multiplied by the percentage of articles in both newspapers that address inter-party relational conflict. If one were to plot a second line, representing the magnitude of intraparty and nonpartisan conflict and party system polarization, it would be a mirror image of the line displayed. Note in the figure 2.5 that both the New Deal of the Franklin Roosevelt presidency and the Great Society programs of the Lyndon Johnson Administration are occurring in the trough displayed in the figure 2.5. The low values suggest that either party polarization or inter-party relational conflict is not extreme or, as likely, both are holding steady at some moderate level. This is the level of interactive legislative conflict that LCT suggests one can expect more productivity.

Note also the dip in the 103rd Congress (1993–1995), President Bill Clinton's first Congress. Interactive conflict reaches its lowest point since the 97th Congress (1981–1983) the first Reagan Administration Congress. We would expect both of these honeymoon Congresses to be among the most productive in the past 40 years. Again, this may occur because of low polarization or inter-party relational, while the other dimension of

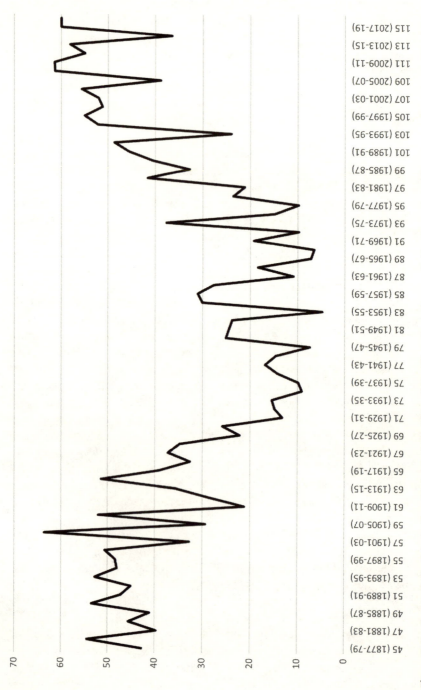

Figure 2.5 Senate Party Polarization * Inter-Party Relational Conflict. *Source:* Compiled by the author, polarization data available at voteview.com, voteview.com/data.

conflict is high. Alternatively, some median level of both types of conflict would produce the same results. To illustrate, if both types of conflict were at hypothetical "5" interactive conflict would equal 25. If one dimension moved to "6" and the other dropped to "4," we would have the same level of conflict. However, if one dimension stayed at "5" and the other soars to "10" we are reaching a high level of interactive conflict, hypothesized to be counter-productive.

Particularly instructive about the use of an interaction term, which blends the two types of conflict, is that this strategy allows for a test of the value of inter-party relational conflict if there was no Senate polarization. Likewise, one can learn something about the value of polarization if there is no inter-party relational conflict. LCT, with its primary focus on the value of moderate conflict, produces postulates regarding these hypothetical scenarios. Specifically, all else being equal, if there was no inter-party relational conflict an increase in Senate polarization should increase legislative productivity. Likewise, if there was no polarization, and the political parties were perfectly undisciplined, a little rabble rousing or inter-party relational conflict ought to help structure policy debate in a way that aids meaningful legislative output. Although zero relational conflict or party polarization are not real-world possibilities, they present an intriguing test of LCT. I will conduct these tests and present the results in chapter 6.

SUMMARY

This chapter has wrestled with a series of thorny measurement issues, not the least of which is an indicator of relational conflict. Using newspaper reporting, it is determined that there have been some personal incivilities throughout the past 140+ years of Congressional history. Certainly, if we could extend the measurement strategy back in time, we would find relational conflict occurring over an even longer period. With the data we have, some Congresses clearly witness more of these relational animosities than others do. The 74th and 83rd Congresses are excellent examples. Notably, relational conflict in the 74th Congress (1935–1937) was ostensibly intraparty and was occurring at a time when the two major political parties were not as polarized as they would become in subsequent eras. Based on LCT, this is a prescription for legislative productivity. Relational conflict increases at a time when party polarization is too low causing moderate conflict, and theoretically, legislative productivity. In all, the partisan nature of relational conflict ought to matter, and intraparty relational conflict ought to help in many instances. Although one must recognize that under conditions of extreme party polarization, any additional relational conflict, of any tenor, is likely problematic.

Although there are many options for measuring party system polarization, and each different measure entails some interesting insights, I have opted for the DW-NOMINATE score differences, which have become a standard-bearer for capturing the phenomenon in much contemporary work on Congress. In order to test a moderation thesis, I have folded the polarization data to produce an indicator of moderate polarization. I also interact Senate polarization with inter-party relational conflict and expect higher numbers will associate with legislative gridlock or stalemate. To test these arguments, it is necessary to settle on an appropriate indicator of legislative achievement, Congress-by-Congress. This is the focus of chapter 4. However, before embarking on this task I would be remiss to skip over a critique I have received many times since embarking on my study of legislative conflict. Many of my contemporaries have suggested that party polarization and relational conflict are the same. One critic noted, "even if they are not the same, there aren't any unique implications."[11] I turn our attention to this possibility in chapter 3.

NOTES

1. Despite some recent consideration and discussion of incivility in the field of legislative studies (Iyengar, Sood, and Lelkes 2012; Skytte 2020), there has been little concerted effort, thus far, to measure the phenomenon directly. Kathleen Hall Jamieson has been among the first to work in this area, and her initial efforts searched the *Congressional Record* for acerbic legislative debate and used counts of certain word usage as a surrogate for incivility (Jamieson 1992; Jamieson and Falk 2000). Following civility retreats in the late 1990s, however, legislators stopped using or dramatically reduced much of the language that Jamieson had been using as a measure of incivility. I suggest this occurred without a corresponding decrease in true levels of relational conflict. Eric Uslaner (1993) attempts to capture incivilities, or breaks in comity, via measures of ideological extremism. My position is that ideological extremism is theoretically and empirically distinct from incivilities. I will test this proposition in chapter 3.

2. Notably, I have used a similar tactic in other published works (Schraufnagel 2005; Dodd and Schraufnagel 2012).

3. To establish inter-coder reliability, two graduate assistants recollected the newspaper articles from 50 of the 144 Congresses in question (30 of 72 from the *Times* and 20 of 72 from the *Post*). The new values representing the number of newspaper articles, Congress by Congress, correlate with the original values at $r = .76$ ($P < .01$). In this subset of cases, I also had the assistants check the nature of the conflict being discussed in the article, whether the conflict was inter-party, intraparty, or nonpartisan, and I obtained an average correlation with the original values of $r = .90$. I examined all differences carefully and ultimately used some of the new information in the measures reported here. I also had a third student redo the 114th Congress for

both newspapers and obtained a correlation of $r = .67$ ($P < .01$) for the *Post* and $r = .74$ for the *Times*. Again, I considered the differences and made some minor changes.

4. Editorial, *New York Times*, March 6, 1935, 1.
5. Editorial, *New York Times*, March 10, 1935, E10.
6. Robert C. Albright, *Washington Post*, June 12, 1954, 1.
7. As a validity check and to control for possible changes in the relative coverage of Congress in the two newspapers, I divide the number of articles mentioning incidents of incivility by the number of articles published in the newspapers during a specific Congress, which contained the words "Congress," "Senate," or "House of Representatives" in the title. I use the precise start and end date for each biennial Congress when conducting this search. The bivariate correlation between the original measure and the measure, which uses the denominator, for the 72th Congresses is $r = .70$ ($P < .001$). The correlation for inter-party incivility is $r = .76$ ($P < .001$) and for intraparty incivility is $r = .41$ ($P < .006$).

Ultimately, I do not use these alternative indicators in the testing in subsequent chapters. The high and statistically significant correlations between the two measurement strategies do provide some validation. I remain open to considering any unique measurement strategies.

8. For a comprehensive list of attempts to measure partisan ideology, including interest group scores, which can then be aggregated to distinguish the parties, *see* Burden, Caldeira, and Groseclose (2000).
9. For more on the peculiarities of the 47th Senate, see the Senates own webpage last accessed July 29, 2023 https://www.senate.gov/about/origins-foundations/parties-leadership/presidents-death-eases-senate-deadlock.htm
10. I do consider the two-chamber average, House, and Senate values when constructing the measure of moderate conflict to use in chapter 6, which provides tests of the moderate conflict thesis relating to legislative productivity. Because there is appreciably no difference in the results obtained, I report results based on the Senate values. Importantly, I am not suggesting in any way that the empirical tests I report will be the definitive model of legislative productivity. Others may want to use a two-chamber average. My intention is, simply, to bring attention to the two-dimensional nature of legislative conflict and the value of moderate conflict.
11. This is a criticism I received when presenting my ideas at the Midwest Political Science Association annual meeting in Chicago in 2004. The critic who rose from his chair and shouted his feedback will remain nameless.

Chapter 3

Party Polarization and Member Incivilities

How Distinct Are the Two Dimensions of Conflict

It is *not* difficult to imagine two members of Congress with polar opposite views on the important issues of our times also not getting along with one another on a personal level. Under this scenario, they vote differently, they never socialize with one another, and they may even berate their ideological opponent in public. A Congress full of these types of toxic relationships certainly might find it difficult to get things done, given the congressional handbag of obstructionist tools, which includes the Senate filibuster. Yet, if there are ever instances when policy rivals get along with one another on a personnel level, perhaps even co-sponsoring legislation, then legislative conflict may be two-dimensional. To be certain, the entire enterprise of this book requires the two forms of conflict to be distinct.

I explore this question in three ways. First, I use an individual level of analysis and take a case study approach, briefly studying the careers of four members of the same political party. I continue with an individual-level analysis and conduct a large-n statistical test. In this second instance, the intention is to test whether ideologically extreme members, those who fuel party system polarization, on average, are more likely to be the same individuals who show up in the newspaper reports as engaging in norm-breaking relational conflict. If they are the same people, I will need to concede that the proposed two dimensions of legislative conflict overlap one another in a significant way and unique implications of each type might be missing. Third, I investigate the possibility of two-dimensional legislative conflict using individual Congresses as the unit of analysis. In this instance, I simply need to plot the values already discussed in chapter 2, and look to see if the two forms of conflict consistently rise and fall together overtime. My hunch is that there will be considerable dissimilarities with implications for an effective legislative process.

CASE STUDIES

My first test of the distinction between the two types of legislative conflict uses a case study approach, examining the legislative careers of four House Republicans from two states. All four members served in the 108th Congress (2003–2005). The 108th experiences considerable party system polarization and the phenomenon of party distinctive voting behavior is on an upward trajectory. I did not choose the four individuals randomly. I chose two of the members because the newspaper articles I have consulted, mentioned them multiple times as being involved in personality battles or norm-breaking ethical lapses, of one sort or another. I then chose two members from their same political party, their same state, their same chamber, and their same Congress, who the newspaper articles never mention as engaging in relational conflict or any type of dishonorable behavior. The members chosen are William Marshall "Bill" Thomas and Dana Rohrabacher from California and Stephen Scott Emory McInnis and Joel Maurice Hefley representatives from the Rocky Mountain State (Colorado). Newspaper accounts suggest that Thomas and McInnis have temper issues and lapses in ethical judgment, and there are no mentions of Rohrabacher or Hefley in any of the newspaper articles.

Thomas and Rohrabacher (California Republicans)

Reporters, at the two newspapers consulted, mention Representative Bill Thomas in five different articles, the first during the 107th Congress and then four more times in the 108th. In the earliest incident, in his role as Chair of the House Ways and Means Committee, his chief nemesis was Charles Rangel (D-NY). The *Times* reports, in 2002, that their relationship has been "fraying for a long time" and that "Mr. Thomas's temper was an issue when he sought the chairmanship in 2000." Fellow Republicans note "he doesn't suffer fools well" and the *Times* reports, "Some Republicans complain about Mr. Thomas's edge."[1]

In the 108th Congress both the *Times* and *Post* cover the incident involving Pete Stark (D-CA) and Scott McInnis (R-CO) and the late-night meeting that stopped just short of a brawl in the corridor between a committee room and the House library. Thomas was at the heart of the meltdown and was the one who called in the Capital Police, asking them to evict the Democrats from the library. Bipartisan observers viewed Thomas's move as ramping up the conflict unnecessarily. The *Post* writes about the incident, "The scorn focused on Thomas, whose self-confidence borders on arrogance and whose abrasive manner has long been tolerated by House leaders."[2] Ultimately, Thomas offers a tearful apology for his part in the late-night fracas. This does not stop the *Washingtonian*, another periodical that follows Congress closely, from scoring Thomas in 2004 as the "hottest temper" in the House. In the survey of congressional staffers, Thomas received double the number of votes from the staff members than the person finishing second (Jim Moran D-VA).[3]

Importantly, Thomas's excessive pride or self-confidence did not simply appear when he became chair of the powerful House Ways and Means Committee. As early as 1992, Thomas was implicated in the House banking scandal, which surfaced when members were caught writing themselves loans, in the form of bad checks, at the House Bank. His *hubris* was also on display in 2001 when accused of having an affair with a lobbyist for pharmaceutical and insurance interests. At the time, he was the chair of the subcommittee that regulated Health Maintenance Organizations. The lobbyist, Deborah Steelman, nor Thomas, ever denied the affair. At the time, in an open letter, Thomas wrote, "Any personal failures of commitment or responsibility to my wife, family or friends are just that, personal."[4] Steelman later became vice president of Eli Lilly and steered very significant campaign contributions to Thomas.

Given Thomas's well-known temperament and acerbic personality, if the two-dimensions of conflict, I have been discussing, are nearly the same or closely related, Representative Thomas should have a high personal DW-NOMINATE score. That is, he should be an ideologue with a voting record more immoderate than the chamber mean. Yet, that is not the case. In the 108th Congress, the chamber mean score is .040, and the Republican Party mean score is .417. Thomas's personal score is .371, somewhat closer to the chamber mean than the party average. His fellow Republican from California, who served in the same Congress, Dana Rohrabacher, received a score of .626 in the 108th Congress, representing more extreme voting behavior than the average Republican. Notably, no one has ever considered Rohrabacher a moderate. He often espoused pro-Russian views and support for Russian President Vladimir Putin. Yet, his name never surfaced in any of the newspaper searches.

Rohrabacher's life before entering Congress is unique. As a graduate student at the University of Southern California in the 1970s, he had side gigs as a folk singer and local journalist. He also served as an assistant press secretary for presidential candidate Ronald Reagan in his 1976 and 1980 presidential campaigns. Subsequently, Rohrabacher was a speechwriter in the Reagan White House for eight years. He first won a House seat in the 1988 election cycle. It seems Rohrabacher's life experiences taught him a certain civility, sufficient for him to avoid personality battles, and the type of norm breaking that ends up in newspapers. All the while, Rohrabacher never seemed to compromise his policy positions and in the ten Congresses in which he served, his voting record was always more extreme than the Republican Party mean. The implication is that one can maintain strong, even extreme, policy positions, while maintaining civil relations in the congressional workplace.

McInnis and Hefley (Republicans from Colorado)

I already mentioned Scott McInnis (R-CO) in chapter 1. He was involved in the late-night collapse in civility, which occurred in a House committee room in 2003, involving Pete Stark (D-CA) and Bill Thomas (R-CA). McInnis was the one who told Stark to "Shut Up!" This was not the only time, however, that McInnis was involved in dubious behavior. In 2004, McInnis was paying his wife for campaign work, from campaign funds, at a time when he was not a candidate for re-election. In 2010, when McInnis was running for governor of Colorado, newspaper reports surfaced accusing him of plagiarism for work he was doing for the Hasan Family Foundation after leaving Congress. Although McInnis has successfully avoided blame in both affairs, his involvement in potential ethical lapses does cause pause. At minimum, the deflecting of culpability in the plagiarism case caused relational conflict with the employee he tried to hold liable. In the end, the plagiarism accusations cause McInnis to drop out of the governor's race.

McInnis was a police officer, hospital director, and lawyer before entering Congress. His relational conflict, involving Pete Stark (D-CA), occurred in his sixth and final term in Congress. Given questions regarding ethical conduct and relational difficulties, one might imagine that McInnis would have contributed to party polarization in the 108th Congress. Yet, again, this is not the case. His DW-NOMINATE score in the 108th Congress was .391, which is closer to the chamber mean than the average Republican. Joel Hefley, another Republican from Colorado serving in the 108th had an ideology score of .591, about 50 percent above the party mean. Thorough scrutiny of newspaper reports of the proceedings of the 108th Congress; however, does not turn up any mention of Hefley engaged in relational conflict or any possible dishonorable behaviors. Notably, Hefley was in Congress the entire time that McInnis, his fellow Coloradan, served, and for quite a few years prior and subsequent to McInnis' service. For the entire time Hefley served, from 1987 to 2007, there is no evidence of norm-breaking incivilities in the sources consulted.

As noted, Hefley was hardly a moderate. Yet, he became chair of the House Ethics Committee and reached national prominence when he chaired the proceedings that led to multiple admonishments of Republican Majority Leader Tom DeLay (R-TX). For his part, newspaper articles implicate DeLay in relational conflict three times in three different Congresses. Before his years in Congress, Hefley served as a management consultant and then executive director of a non-profit organization focused on community development. This background suggests a certain civic mindedness of the type that one might expect all elected representatives should enlist and retain. Still more, when Hefley's long time aid and hand-chosen successor for his House seat, Jeff Crank, was the subject of a smear campaign by the Christian Coalition of Colorado in the Republican Party primary, in 2006, Hefley, on principle, refused to endorse the eventual Republican nominee. As evidenced by Representative Hefley's career, again, it seems one can maintain a very conservative voting record while upholding principled standards.

I intended these brief sketches of House Republicans, serving in the 108th Congress, to be instructive. Because a member is implicated in relational conflict, it does not suggest they will be more ideological, or in these cases, more conservative. Indeed, there are party members from the same state, serving in the same Congress, who are more conservative and never implicated in relational conflict. I confessed upfront that I did not choose these four members randomly. The intention with the case studies was to explore the possibility that uncivil members are not the same people responsible for the significant party polarization that characterizes twenty-first century Congresses. My claim is that if there is ever an instance where an uncivil member is more moderate, on average, we have come a long way toward establishing two-dimensional legislative conflict. Yet, one can do better. What happens if I match all 431 members implicated in the newspaper reports, over 144 years of congressional history, randomly with someone from their same political party, their same chamber, and their same Congress? Now, there is a large sample size and one can run t-tests for a statistically significant difference in mean DW-NOMINATE scores. Will those members implicated in norm-breaking incivility have more extreme ideology scores, on average, than a randomly chosen matched pair? I turn to this test next.

ARE UNCIVIL MEMBERS POLICY EXTREMISTS: A LARGE-N ANALYSIS

As noted, in the 144 years of newspaper coverage, I turn up 431 members of Congress implicated in relational conflict. This equates to an average of about three members a year or six members per Congress. Notably, only the 93rd Congress (1973–1975) had no implicated members. This was the Congress seated during the Watergate hearings focused on the wrongdoings of President Richard Nixon. It seems the focus on the president's misdeeds was sufficient to keep members of Congress from berating each other publicly.

Seven other Congresses had only one member implicated. Of the 431 implicated members, from seventy-two Congresses, 208 are senators and 223 are members of the House of Representatives. The large number of senators, given a much smaller chamber size, suggests reporters may be paying closer attention to the Upper Chamber. Considering party affiliation, 215 members are Democrats, 206 are Republicans, and 10 were members of minor parties.

For these tests, I use a matched pair analysis, which is a type of Most Similar Case Design. Specifically, I match each implicated member with someone chosen randomly from his or her same political party, chamber, and Congress. The only consideration is that the matched pair be someone the newspaper reports never implicated in relational conflict or ethical lapses. For instance, in the 104th Congress (1995–1997) there were five implicated members, all of whom served in the House of Representatives. Two members were Democrats and three were Republicans. To find a matched pair, I use a random number generator, choose two Democrats from the group of 206 party members who served in the 104th Congress and then choose three Republicans from the 237 party members serving in the 104th. I use random selection with replacement. If a chosen individual was an implicated member or a matched pair who was already in the sample, I place that person's name back in the pool and choose a new number.

This process nets a sample of 862 members representing seventy-one of the seventy-two Congresses studied. Newspaper reporters had implicated half of the group. The other half serves as a control group. The Most Similar Case Design will hold constant political party, legislative chamber, and the time period the members served. Matching on these three qualities assures that none of these factors can explain why newspaper reports implicated some members and not others. Notably, considering the ten minor party members, I was able to match eight of them with someone from their same political party. In two cases, it was necessary to match the implicated member with someone from a different minor party because they were the only person from their political party serving in Congress at that time. I end up pairing William Mahone, a Virginian from the Readjuster Party, with David Davis, an Independent Party member from Illinois. Both served in the 47th Congress (1881–1883). In the second instance, Victor Berger from Wisconsin was the only Socialist serving in the 62nd House of Representatives (1911–1913) and I paired him with Ira Copley, a Progressive Party member from Illinois.

What I wish to test is whether ideological extremism associates with implicated members. In other words, are the implicated members contributing more to party system polarization than randomly chosen members from the same political party? If they are, then the two dimensions of conflict I have been discussing are related. To test this, I use individual DW-NOMINATE scores. It is important to recognize that the chamber and party average values of party polarization, discussed in the previous chapter, use individual member scores to create averages. In the tests, I use individual member scores and calculate Congress averages for the two groups: implicated members and their matched pairs. I then compare each group's average score to the chamber mean score, in the relevant Congress.

Most specifically, I calculate the absolute value of the average difference from the chamber mean for each group. These average differences are the focus of the testing. If our implicated members are ideologues, fueling party polarization, they should have scored further from the chamber mean score. One can test this in several different ways. I began by lumping everyone together ($n = 862$), which has the disadvantage of mixing House and Senate polarization scores. However, I then examine just House members and just senators. I also test for difference using only House Republicans, House Democrats, Senate Republicans, and Senate Democrats. The intention is to make sure I am not missing something. The lack of a difference between the two groups when considering the entire sample might be masking chamber or party-specific findings.

Table 3.1 reports the results, which compare average group scores. Considering the entire sample size, at the top of the table ($n = 862$), which lumps House and Senate members, the median difference for the entire sample is .3544. Note the 431 implicated members have a slightly lower difference (.3527) than the Congress average score and their matched pairs have a slightly higher average score (.3561). This suggests that the uncivil members, on average, are less extreme in their voting behavior.

Moving to the test that separates the two chambers, I learn the difference score for the whole House ($n = 446$) equals .3873. In this case, the uncivil members have a slightly higher average difference (.3997; $n = 223$) than the matched pairs (.3850; $n = 223$). Yet, when we move to the Senate, the implicated members have a slightly lower mean difference than the control group. Importantly, none of the differences appears very large. In fact, as we break things down further and examine the four party/chamber-specific tests, we learn that in all instances the difference in means for the two groups is quite small. In three of these four tests, the implicated group does have a higher number; however, in the fourth instance (Senate Republicans), the matched pair group has the higher number, indicating more extreme voting behavior. Importantly, it is possible to test whether any of the differences between the two groups reach standard acceptable levels of statistical significance.

In table 3.1, I uncovered no obvious evidence that members implicated in relational conflict, on average, are more immoderate in their voting behavior. By extension, there is no evidence that party polarization and incivility are the same phenomenon. In table 3.2, I provide the results of t-tests to determine

Table 3.1   Measuring the Difference in Ideology Scores Implicated Members and Their Matched Pair: Comparing each Group to the Chamber Mean Score (45th–116th Congress)

Sample Mean Difference* = .3544	
Implicated Members .3527	Matched Pairs .3561
House Mean Difference = .3873	Senate Mean Difference = .3191
House-Implicated .3897 / House-Matched Pair .3850	Senate-Implicated .3130 / Senate-Matched Pair .3251
House DEM Mean Difference = .3582	House GOP Mean Difference = .4172
House DEM-Implicated .3601 / House DEM-Matched Pair .3564	House GOP-Implicated .4200 / House GOP-Matched Pair .4145
Senate DEM Mean Difference = .3418	Senate GOP Mean Difference = .2920
Senate DEM-Implicated .3442 / Senate DEM-Matched Pair .3393	Senate GOP-Implicated .2759 / Senate GOP-Matched Pair .3082

Source: Compiled by the Author from data available at https://voteview.com/static/data/out/members/HSall_members.csv
DEM = Democratic Party; GOP = Republican Party
* All "Difference" values are the absolute value of the difference in DW-NOMINATE scores for the group(s) identified.

Table 3.2   The Absolute Value of the Difference in Mean DW-NOMINATE Scores: Implicated Members vs. Matched Pairs (45th–116th Congress)

Group	Implicated vs. Matched Pair t-statistic for Difference in Means
Sample ($n = 862$)	.269
House Sample ($n = 446$)	-.279
Senate Sample ($n = 416$)	.635
House Democrats Sample ($n = 226$)	-.155
House Republicans Sample ($n = 220$)	-.249
Senate Democrats Sample ($n = 226$)	-.176
Senate Republicans Sample ($n = 190$)	1.302

Source: Compiled by the Author from data available at https://voteview.com/static/data/out/members/HSall_members.csv
Note: A negative t-statistic suggests implicated members have a higher mean difference.

whether any of the differences in mean scores for the two groups will reach standard levels of statistical significance. Put differently, the t-tests will more completely determine whether the implicated members are, on average, in any way systematically and statistically significantly different from the control group. Given the large sample sizes, one only needs a t-statistic of about

1.645 to be reasonably confident that there is a relevant difference between the two groups.

Note in table 3.2 none of the tests approach the definition of statistical difference. Put simply, the voting behavior of implicated members is indistinguishable from the voting behavior of the control group. I uncover no evidence that uncivil members are contributing in a systematic manner to party system polarization. Still more, the only t-test that returns a value greater than "1" is the test for Senate Republicans. In this instance, the finding suggests the control group has more extreme voting behavior. Albeit, the difference does not quite reach standard levels of statistical significance.

TESTING FOR TWO-DIMENSIONAL CONFLICT: CONGRESS-BY-CONGRESS

This chapter began with the proposition that one ought to look carefully for any evidence that conflict in Congress is unidimensional. If the two types of conflict discussed overlap in a major way, there may not be unique implications. In the case studies of four Republicans serving in the 108th Congress (2003–2005), I first uncover evidence that the two modes of conflict can certainly deviate from one another. The two members with more ideological, or extreme, voting tendencies did not engage in relational conflict. The two more moderate members did. Importantly, in the large-n analysis, the research has uncovered evidence that those who engage in relational conflict, on average, are *not* ideologues who fuel party system polarization. Next, I will use each Congress as the unit of analysis and see if it is possible to determine whether there have been times when the two types of conflict are mutually reinforcing? Conversely, are there historical periods when the two modes of conflict diverge from one another?

Figure 3.1 presents these results. I have standardized the values for the two types of conflict for the sake of presentation (subtracted the mean and divided by the standard deviation for each observation). Moreover, once I obtained the standardized values, for each Congress, I added "2" to each observation to remove negative values. Again, I do this for the sake of presentation. The manipulations for display purposes aside, the reader will recognize the patterns in figure 3.1 from chapter 2. These are the same values presented earlier, now however, they are on the same scale and presented in the same figure.

Looking at the pattern for relational conflict, there is a sort of parallel waved motion with Senate polarization. Incivility in Congress reached a heightened peak in the late nineteenth century, with standardized incivility scores roughly parallel with standardized Senate polarization scores, except relational conflict is showing more variation. Personality conflict then declines,

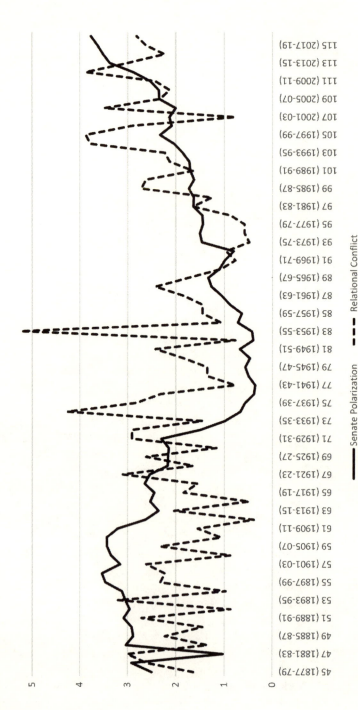

Figure 3.1 Comparing Senate Polarization and Relational Conflict: 45th–116th Congresses. *Source:* Compiled by the author, polarization data available at voteview.com, voteview.com/data.

reaching its low ebb in the mid-twentieth century, and moves upward in the late twentieth century, again, consistent with the party polarization measure. Yet, there are important differences. The early decline of incivility began well before the decline of polarization, so that from the William McKinley Administration until Woodrow Wilson's last 66th Congress (1919–1921), incivility in standardized terms is always below the standardized polarization scores. Then as the party system greatly depolarizes in the New Deal era, incivility in standardized terms remains well above the standardized polarization scores until the Richard Nixon Administration. In the Nixon and Jimmy Carter Administrations, both polarization and incivility are in the moderately depolarized and moderately uncivil range, thereafter moving upward roughly together until the administration of George W. Bush and the terrorist strikes of September 11, 2001. However, please note the saw-toothed pattern of relational conflict, throughout, that is clearly missing in the polarization timeline.

The differentiations between the incivility and polarization scores are critically important to the analysis of effective legislative process, which will be the focus of chapter 6. While there is some substantial parallelism between the two types of conflict, there are also substantial periods when incivility in standardized terms is substantially lower than polarization during the polarized Congresses of the Progressive Era (1897–1920). This patterning holds out the possibility that lower incivility is somewhat defusing polarized conflict, the conditions that I argue are essential to a productive legislature in polarized settings. Similarly, there are substantial periods when incivility in standardized terms ranges well above the low standardized polarization scores found amidst the depolarized Congress of the mid-twentieth century. This patterning holds out the possibility that higher levels of incivility helped foster sufficient policy engagement and contestation to generate productivity even amidst weak or modest party conflict.

Last, in a close analysis of figure 3.1, one can notice valleys in relational conflict related to presidential honeymoons or the first Congress of a newly elected president. Scholars have long established that a president's first Congress tends to be more productive (Mayhew 1991; Edwards III, Barrett, and Peake 1997; Coleman 1999; Binder 2003). Perhaps there is a dip in relational conflict as members of Congress seek to give the new president the benefit of the doubt, putting their personal grudges aside, temporarily. Perhaps it is this tempering of conflict, which allows for effective contestation of innovative policy proposals and prompts legislative productivity in honeymoon Congresses. I will provide tests, which consider this proposition in chapter 6.

Of course, my arguments about the interplay of relational conflict and polarization look beyond the general patterns of incivility. I suggest the most critical factor for policy productivity is the way in which the partisan character of relational conflict interacts with party polarization. Specifically,

I hold, in polarized contexts inter-party incivility is the great threat to policy productivity, inflaming conflict in ways that will hinder innovation, whereas the presence or absence of intraparty incivility should be relatively unimportant. In depolarized settings, intraparty incivility is likely to be the critical energizing force generating productivity, whereas the presence or absence of inter-party incivility should be less important. Thus, a critical issue is not so much the timing of general patterns of relational conflict but rather the timing of partisan patterns of incivility, in interaction with party polarization. More on this in chapter 6.

SUMMARY

This chapter has provided a robust test of the two-dimensional conflict thesis, which is integral to LCT. Although I have been discussing two-dimensional legislative conflict for nearly thirty years, it was rare, until recently, for my peers to accept that incivility and party polarization are distinct. When these scholars were willing to accept that, theoretically, they could be distinct, their consolation was always conditional and followed by the caution that it is not possible to measure incivility or that there are unlikely any unique implications. The first rebuke remains salient. I have developed an indicator of incivility with some face validity. Yet, one must always be looking to improve on measurement strategies in the social sciences. It is my hope that others will follow up and provide better indicators of individual level, and Congress specific, norm-breaking relational conflict.[5] To address the second warning, it is necessary to develop indicators of an effective legislative process or legislative productivity, and this is the subject of chapter 5.

For now, I would like to suggest that I have uncovered reasonable evidence that the two forms of legislative conflict are not just theoretically distinct, but empirically dissimilar. If uncivil members, willing to engage in relational conflict, were the same people fueling party system polarization, this would be relatively easy to uncover. Their voting behavior, on average, would be more distinct. Yet, this is not the case. Moreover, considering Congress-by-Congress values of the two types of conflict, polarization moves more smoothly overtime. Relational conflict has significant peaks and valleys. A couple of peaks in the 1930s and 1950s were the result of the antics of two senators (Huey Long and Joseph McCarthy), and the valley, representing the 107th Congress occurs in the aftermath of international terrorist incidents. Yet, there is more movement, in incivility, to consider.

In chapter 4, I will consider the backgrounds of implicated members. Specifically, I seek to test whether there are systematic explanations for why some members behave uncivilly while others do not. This is a tall order and a comprehensive test would likely involve careful scrutiny of the psychology of members. I will not provide this type of analysis or any definitive answers. However, I do hope to initiate the conversation. The scholarly community now has a list of 431 members who have engaged in mean-spirited norm-breaking behaviors. A deep dive into their personalities with a control group ought to turn up something. Political scientists have begun using the Big 5 Personality Traits of Psychology to help us understand political phenomena (De Neve 2015; Lyons et al. 2016; Weinschenk and Dawes 2017) and there is great promise here as it relates to the norm-breaking behaviors of members of Congress. Chapter 4 will provide a starting point for this discussion. Notably, it is important to remember that norm-breakers in certain periods may be helpful to the legislative process, especially if we are in a depolarized era defined by cross-party collusion. In the third decade of the twenty-first century, defined by intense conflict of all sorts, the country could certainly benefit from the recruitment of more civil members.

NOTES

1. Robin Toner, *New York Times*, July 1, 2002, A12.
2. Juliet Eilperin, *Washington Post*, July 24, 2023, A1.
3. *Washingtonian*, at https://www.washingtonian.com/2004/09/01/best-worst-of-congress/ (last accessed September 11, 2023).
4. Nick Anderson, *Los Angeles Times*, June 27, 2000, https://www.latimes.com/archives/la-xpm-2000-jun-27-mn-45289-story.html (last accessed September 11, 2023).
5. Some scholars have begun to look at individual norm breaking using offensive tweets (Frimer et al. 2022), the interruption of speakers (Miller and Sutherland 2022), and grandstanding during committee hearings (Park 2021).

Chapter 4

What Explains Uncivil Member Behavior?

Given the hyper-two-dimensional conflict of the 2020s, it is easy to embrace the notion that all conflict is bad and that we need to find people to serve in government with the ability to compromise on policy and get along with one another on a personal level. Certainly, that perspective is a reasonable proposition for the third decade of the twenty-first century. However, one ought not to assume that present day circumstances will never change. Moreover, we know that in the 1940s and 1950s across party cooperation, indicative of too little meaningful legislative conflict, was able to prevent movement in the policy areas of civil rights and the environment, along with other pertinent matters. Arguably, there is still considerable elite collusion and avoidance that leave important sociopolitical topics unaddressed. For instance, no one in elite circles seems to be seriously entertaining banking or airline regulation. Two industries that almost routinely require taxpayer bailouts of one sort or another. Moreover, comprehensive immigration policy has been seemingly impossible in twenty-first century Congresses. Perhaps we need a rabble-rouser of the Huey Long (D-LA) variety to help supply meaningful policy alternatives.

Authoritarian regimes, throughout the ages, persist because of suppressed political discussion and dialogue. The present-day United States may also suffer from stifled debate on key issues. It is important to remember that uncivil members have not always been bad for the legislative process or the good of the country. This seems to, especially, be the case when they direct their animosities toward members of their own political party. This has the potential to create cleavages of a sort, sufficient to produce majority support for meaningful policy change. The incivilities of Huey Long (D-LA) in the 1930s were arguably productive because his populist program prescriptions were normally more progressive than the policies proposed by the Franklin

D. Roosevelt Administration. This had the effect of legitimizing Roosevelt's proposals, making them seem more moderate and reasonable.

The countervailing normative implications of relational conflict in different eras aside, it makes sense to learn more about the rabble-rousers. Who are they? In chapter 3, a database with 431 implicated members and their matched pairs was established. I cull a list of the 186 members of Congress whom newspaper reporters mention in more than one article as engaging in norm-breaking incivilities, while serving in Congress. The names of the members appear in Appendix A. I do not intend this to be a "wall of shame." To reiterate, some of the rebels arguably served an important function in helping to structure meaningful policy debate. Moreover, we must appreciate the need for political conflict in an open society. On the other hand, some implicated members clearly were unhelpful, and their congressional service was a net negative. This especially occurs when there is already sufficient party system polarization to produce meaningful policy choices for members to debate. In the twenty-first century, mean-spirited antagonists are not likely serving any useful purpose.

When pulling the names from the newspaper articles, I was initially concerned about two considerations. First, I worried that members implicated in newspaper articles once, and only once, might not be very different from those members who the newspapers never mention. Undoubtedly, there have always been a few members engaged in overt relational conflict with colleagues, who do not catch the attention of newspaper reporters. Others, by the luck of the draw, were reasonably civil throughout their time in Congress with the one exception, or one instance, when they happened to catch the attention of a reporter at either the *New York Times* or *Washington Post*. I address this concern in two ways.

In the database that holds the names of both groups of legislators, the uncivil members and their matched pair, I create a dependent variable labeled *Multiple Mentions* and score cases "1" if more than one newspaper article mentions the member during their congressional service. Of the 431 implicated members, newspaper reporters mentioned 186 of them multiple times. In a few instances, multiple articles covered the same relational conflict episode, and I still use these individuals under the assumption that their personal battle was sufficiently serious that it stayed in the news for more than a single day. This smaller group becomes the focus of one of the tests.

Next, I create a dependent variable labeled *Count*, which equals the number of times the newspaper articles mention a member. All 431 members of the control group are scored "0," the 243 members who were mentioned only once are scored "1," and the 186 members with multiple mentions receive a score equal to their number of mentions. For instance, Huey Long (R-LA) and Joseph McCarthy (R-WI) receive scores of "18" and "30," respectively.

Only Benjamin Tillman (D-SC) surpasses Long and McCarthy with thirty-two mentions. After "0" and "1," the most common number of mentions is "2," representing eighty-one members.

Regarding my second initial concern, I worried that newspaper reporters were more likely to closely follow the antics or behaviors of the more newsworthy leaders in Congress than they would rank-and-file members. This concern did not worry me as much when establishing incivility Congress-by-Congress. In that case, I assume that leader incivility is more important and leaders engaged in relational conflict are more "defining" as it relates to the overall level of relational conflict in a Congress. Historically, the power of leaders has vacillated, yet we know that leader assertiveness and commitment to comity have helped to define the legislative process throughout congressional history (Owens, Schraufnagel, and Li 2016). There certainly is considerable attention paid to political party leaders by congressional observers (Jessee and Malhotra 2010; Bendix and MacKay 2017). It seems natural that newspaper reporters would more closely scrutinize leaders' behaviors. Importantly, I do not believe congressional leaders are more likely to engage in relational conflict. Instead, I worry that when trying to understand more about the implicated members, it is necessary to control for the nature of newspaper reporting, which likely focuses disproportionately on congressional leaders.

To account for this, I create two independent or control variables. The first, I label *Party Leader* and the second *Committee Chair*. I score cases in the database "1," on the Leader variable if the implicated member was speaker of the House, president pro tempore of the Senate, or one of the majority and minority leaders or whips in either chamber of Congress. I score all other cases "0." In the second instance, I score implicated members "1" if they were the chair of a subcommittee or standing committees, including the joint committees, in either chamber at any time while they served in Congress. Among the implicated members, 34 of them held one of the leadership positions and 155 of them were a chair during their time in Congress. Considering the randomly selected control group, 15 were leaders and 103 were committee chairs.

THE TESTS

Dependent variables and important control variables aside, I forge forward to see if there is anything more substantively interesting that we can learn about the antagonists. Are there any systematic background considerations they have in common? Given the large swath of congressional history, I am considering, this is a tall order. First, I create a variable called *Party Maverick*. Given the frequency of *intraparty* incivilities or relational conflicts, it might be that, on average, the implicated members do not always support the party line as established by their party leaders. In other words, it might be that uncivil members are mavericks. We already know, from chapter 3, implicated members are not more conservative or liberal, on average, than their party colleagues, when considering the chamber mean DW-NOMINATE score. Recall that, overall, the implicated member's ideology scores were closer to the chamber mean than their matched pair. However, perhaps implicated members are more likely to deviate from their party's mean preference. Perhaps they are more willing, than control group members, to break with their party leaders' preferred positions?

For the entire sample of 862 members, I calculate the absolute value of the difference between each member's ideology score and their party mean score, in the relevant Congress. The implicated members now may be more liberal or conservative but the reference point has changed. Now, a larger number simply indicates the member's policy preferences deviate more from the party mean than his or her matched pair. If so, I label them a "maverick." We know that for William Mahone (VA), the lone Readjuster Party member serving in the 47th Congress (1881–1883) and Victor Berger (WI), the lone Socialist Party member serving in the 62nd Congress (1911–1913) the variable score will be "0." Because their ideology scores are, their party's mean score.

If implicated members are Party Mavericks, I anticipate a statistically significant positive association between this variable and both the Multiple Mentions and Count-dependent variables. I can note that in the first instance, there is a statistically significant bivariate relationship between the maverick consideration and the Multiple Mentions consideration ($r = .10$; $P < .004$; $n = 862$). Considering the Count variable, the bivariate relationship is not quite as strong ($r = .06$; $P < .09$; $n = 862$). Of course, we can easily imagine a possible strong negative relationship between the Party Maverick variable and both the Leader and Chair variables. Their unwillingness to vote with their co-partisans defines their "maverick" status. Once controlling for the party leadership considerations and other factors explained below, we will know more about whether implicated members are more likely to vote against the party's mean preference than a randomly selected control group.

Next, I check whether members of the sample, representing 144 years of congressional history, have experience as state legislators. I hypothesize that members with state legislative experience will associate with a lower likelihood of relational incivilities. Members with greater state legislative experience ought to be more familiar with the principles of lawmaking and more accepting of the practice and decorum of congressional governance, including responsibility for enacting legislation through reciprocity arrangements, compromise, logrolling, coalition-building, and so forth (Mason 1938;

Fenno 1997). Research reported by Michael Berkman shows that when state legislators enter the U.S. House with considerable legislative experience and prowess, they are better able to adapt quickly and well to chamber life and are "better prepared in the personal aspects of legislative politics" (1993, 87). One House member's comment quoted by Berkman applies directly to relational conflict: "[former state legislators] learn that when you insult somebody you are going to regret it later on" (1993, 87).

I follow the lead of Berkman (1993) and code former *State Legislators*, with five or more years of experience "1" and all other members in the sample "0." In this case, I expect a negative coefficient or relationship with each of the two dependent variables. In other words, I hold members with state legislative experience will be less likely to have Multiple Mentions and a lower overall Count. I believe five or more years of state legislative experience is an appropriate cut point. The assumption is that an individual serving more than a single four-year term, or two two-year terms, will have been a member of the state legislature long enough to absorb and appreciate at least some of the norms of the legislative process in an open society. Considering the sample of 862 members, 146 of the members have five or more years of state legislative experience. Of these, the newspaper reports implicate sixty-five of them, and eighty-one members are from the control group. I also test this consideration using the total number of years members served in state legislatures and a third consideration, which tapped whether members served more than two years. I obtain roughly the same result regardless of the measurement strategy. However, a fourth variable scored "1" if the members ever served in a state legislature does not comport with a decreased likelihood of implication in the newspaper reports. This suggests that before members fully appreciate the norms of a democratic legislative process, including norms of deference and reciprocity, it takes some timeserving in a state legislature.

Next, I test for a regional effect by tapping the unique regional political subculture and style of the South. From one perspective, some see the South as purveying an aristocratic political culture that represents the epitome of gentility, courtesy, kindliness, and ease, embodied in heroes like George Washington, James Madison, and Thomas Jefferson. Many analysts, however, have rejected this idea, instead emphasizing the region's embrace of popular religion, and the ill-mannered nature of much of southern politics, but also the relationship between violence and honor in early Southern societies (Cash 1941). Scholars recognize that in the South, men had to defend liberty and honor, lest they have neither (Bertram 1986; Nisbett and Cohen 1996). I create a variable *Southern* and use the same coding rule as *Congressional Quarterly*, a privately owned publishing company that produces several publications that report on congressional activities. Specifically, I code members of Congress from the eleven states of the former confederacy, Kentucky, and

Oklahoma as *Southern*. This nets 274 members of the total sample of 862 members. Newspaper reports implicate 147 of them in relational conflict and 127 appear in the randomly selected control group.

Last, I control for gender. Scholars note that a gender gap exists in American politics and the gap holds over time and across the different regions of the United States (Norrander 1997; Inglehart and Norris 2000). While there is good research, readily available, that finds women, on average, more liberal leaning (Conover and Sapiro 1993; Sapiro and Conover 1997; Box-Steffensmeier, De Boef and Lin 2004), not surprisingly there is little research assessing a gender gap in terms of relational conflict. This will arguably be the first such test and, as such, the test is largely exploratory, with no specific expectation. I can note that of the 862 members in the sample, 29 of them are female. Eleven of these are in the implicated group and 18 are in the control group. Given these numbers, the variable *Female* may be negatively associated, in regression runs, with both the Multiple Mentions and Count dependent variables.

Considering statistical modeling and the first dependent variable, Multiple Mentions, I have a dependent variable that takes on only one of two values. I score cases in the sample "1" if the member is mentioned in newspaper reports multiple times and "0" otherwise. Hence, it is prudent to use a Logistical Regression for multivariate testing. Scholars recommend Logistic Regression when trying to explain binary outcomes (Long 1997). Specifically, the model predicts the probability of an outcome, in this case, implicated or not implicated, by analyzing the relationship between the dependent variable and the explanatory variables included in the model.[1] In the second model, I use a Poisson Regression because the dependent variable is a count of incidences. A Poisson Regression uses a log transformation of the dependent variable, which adjusts for the skewed quality of a count variable.[2] This transformation prevents the model from producing negative predicted values, which are not possible when considering the number of times newspaper reporters implicate a member in relational conflict.

RESULTS

In table 4.1, one can learn which of the independent variables associates with multiple newspaper mentions. In a Logit Regression, one must convert the coefficients back to predicted probabilities to gain a substantive understanding of the effect that the statistically significant variables have on the dependent variable. In table 4.2, I present the results of the Poisson Regression run. Rather than presenting the Poisson coefficients, I provide Incidence Rate Ratios (IRR), which is another way to make more sense of the findings. In the database, I label each of the American states with a number and in

Table 4.1 Testing the Association between Different Considerations and the Probability that the Newspapers Mention a Member Multiple Times as Engaging in Relational Conflict (45th–116th Congress)

	Model: Logit Regression, Standard Errors adjusted for Clusters in 50 States	
Explanatory Variables	Exp. Sign	Logit Coefficient (robust standard error)
Party Maverick	+	2.423 (.673) ***
State Legislator (5+ years)	-	-.540 (.243) *
Southerner	+	.065 (.192)
Female	-	-1.268 (.651) *
Control Variables		
Party Leader	+	1.470 (.332) ***
Committee Chair	+	.733 (.182) ***
Constant		-1.908 (.133) ***
Wald Chi^2		68.79 ***
Pseudo R^2		.06
n		862

Source: All data collected and results compiled by the author.
*** $P < .001$; * $P < .05$ (one-tailed tests)

Table 4.2 Testing the Association between Different Considerations and the Count of Newspaper Articles that Mention a Member Engaged in Relational Conflict (45th–116th Congress)

	Model: Poisson Regression, Standard Errors adjusted for Clusters in 50 States	
Explanatory Variables	Exp. Sign	Incident Rate Ratios
Party Maverick	+	3.252
State Legislator (5+ years)	-	.599
Southerner	+	1.417
Female	-	.608
Control Variables		
Party Leader	+	2.231
Committee Chair	+	1.967
Constant		.676
Wald Chi^2		92.60 ***
n		862

Source: All data collected and results compiled by the author.
*** $P < .001$; All variables are statistically significant in the expected direction (one-tailed tests)

the model runs; I cluster the error term by state. This will provide a more robust test of statistical significance and help to alleviate concerns about the autocorrelation of the errors occurring as a result of multiple members in the database serving in Congress from the same state. I can note that without this check, the relationship between the explanatory variables and the dependent variables is much stronger, which indicates that autocorrelation of errors is indeed present.

In table 4.1, one can note straightaway a statistically significant link between all but one of the explanatory variables and the dependent variable, the exception is the variable Southern. In this instance, members from the South do not associate with a greater likelihood of multiple implications in the newspaper articles consulted. Especially interesting, I learned there is a statistical link, on average, between the Party Maverick consideration and the probability the newspapers will have implicated a member more than once. Specifically, the distance between each member's voting behavior, as captured by their DW-NOMINATE score, and the party mean score is associated with an increase in the probability of engaging in relational conflict. Even more specifically, members whose voting behavior is closest to the party mean associate with about a 13 percent probability of appearing in multiple articles and this grows to an almost 49 percent probability for members whose voting behavior is most distinct from the party mean. Put simply, Party Mavericks are engaging in more relational conflict, on average, all else being equal, across the 144 years of congressional history studied.

Importantly, this is not the same as saying that Party Mavericks are ideologues. We learned that implicated members are not extreme in their voting behavior, relative to the chamber mean. As it turns out, our implicated members are often closer to the chamber mean than their matched pair. However, the distance from the party mean, considering both groups, does associate with an increase in the probability of engaging in relational conflict. In unidimensional space, one can imagine a scenario like the one displayed in figure 4.1. The figure shows the relative position of House Republicans, based on the empirical tests conducted. The implicated members are at position b. in the figure and their matched pairs are at position c. The model run suggests the control group is statistically significantly closer to the party mean than

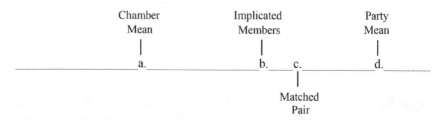

Figure 4.1 Implicated Members and their Ideology, Relative to Chamber and Party Means. *Source*: Illustration by the author.

the implicated members are. However, as we learned in chapter 3, the implicated members are often closer to the chamber mean. Although, in the latter instance, the difference between the two groups did not reach standard levels of statistical significance.

Notably, Party Leaders and Committee Chairs are also more likely to appear in the newspaper reports multiple times. Unfortunately, it is difficult to argue that leaders and chairs are more likely to be uncivil. The strong suspicion is that the newspaper reporters at the *Times* and *Post* simply follow these members more closely and are more prone to scrutinize their personal interactions. Considering the negative coefficients in table 4.1, we learn that both State Legislators and Females are less likely to be uncivil, on average, after controlling for the other considerations. Specifically, considering members with five or more years' service in state legislators the modeling suggests these individuals will have a little less than an 11 percent probability of multiple mentions and this grows to slightly more than a 17 percent probability for members without the level of state legislative experience considered. Reflecting on gender, there is about a 17 percent probability that the newspapers will implicate men as uncivil multiple times, and the probability drops to less than 6 percent for female members. In the contemporary era, defined by hyper-partisanship and relational conflict, we learn that recruiting former state legislators and women might help reduce the overall amount of conflict in Congress and move average conflict to a more moderate level, a level capable of producing legislative successes and avoiding gridlock.

In table 4.2, I report the results of the test, which uses the Count of relational conflict articles found in the newspapers consulted. The reason for this second test is that often in the social sciences, the results obtained from a particular test are sensitive to measurement and modeling decisions. To check myself and to try to falsify the results obtained from the first model, I run a second test. Now, instead of thinking in terms of an increase or decrease in the predicted probability of implication, we can consider the rate in which the incidence of implication occurs, on average, for members representing the different groups. Note that in this second test, I find all variables included in the model statistically linked to the count of incidences (articles). The large number of articles that address the relational conflicts of Huey Long (D-LA) and Benjamin Tillman (D-SC), two senators from the South, likely pushes the Southern consideration into statistical significance.

When interpreting the results of a Poisson Regression, it makes sense to use the IRR values. For instance, the IRR of 3.252 for the Party Maverick consideration suggests, on average, a one-unit increase in the distance between a member's ideology score and the party mean score increases the rate ratio of appearing in one of the newspaper articles by about 3.3 times, on average, all else being equal. The range of the ideological distance indicator is .768 (Min. Value = 0.0 and Max. Value = .768), so it is necessary to reduce the rate ratio some (3.252 * .768 = 2.50). The "real-world" scenario suggests the member farthest from the party mean score is about 2.5 times more likely to appear in one of the articles, on average, than the member who is closest to the party mean. We know the ones closest to their party mean are minor party members from the 47th and 62nd Congresses. The person furthest from his party mean is Richard Pettigrew (R-SD) who served as a senator from the Mount Rushmore State from the 51st (1889–1891) to the 56th (1899–1901) Congress.

Senator Pettigrew's story is worth telling because it helps make sense of the findings just discussed as it relates to being a "Party Maverick." Pettigrew appears in three different newspaper articles, once in the *Times* during the 54th Congress and twice (once in each newspaper) in the 56th Congress. In the second instance, Pettigrew was in a tussle with fellow Republican Marcus Hanna (R-OH). The relational conflict was sufficient for the "debate" to appear in both newspapers. The *Times* writes, "The sensational criminations and recriminations, for bitter personalities, and for violent invective the debate exceeded anything heard on the floor of the Chamber for many years."[3] Pettigrew was suggesting that Hanna was taking bribes from a shipbuilder interested in government contracts. Notably, Pettigrew, a Republican, in the 56th Congress had a negative DW-NOMINATE score (-.371), which was very close to the Democratic Party mean (-.364) and far from his own party's mean score (.397). Relative to fellow Republicans, Pettigrew was a moderate and certainly did nothing to contribute to party polarization. Yet, he certainly engaged in relational conflict. In the article from the 54th Congress, Pettigrew was in an inter-party tussle with David Hill (D-NY). Specifically, he was leveling excoriating criticisms of New Englanders, in general, for their treatment of Native Americans.

Considering other findings obtained in the Poisson Regression, one can argue that, on average, the likelihood that a member would appear in one of the newspapers would decrease by a factor of nearly .6 (.599) if they had five or more years of experience as a state legislator. A similar decrease is associated with being a female member (.608). The implications of these findings are considerable. If living in a time of hyper-conflict, where any increase in conflict, of any ilk, is likely detrimental to the effective functioning of a legislature, the finding suggest that an increase in former state legislators and women serving in Congress would be a net positive as it relates to moderating conflict. If the goal were to reduce overall conflict, it would be best if members were to complete an "internship" by previously serving in a lower-level legislature. A natural extension of this argument, which goes untested here, is that members of Congress who previously served as congressional staff will be less likely to engage in relational conflict. These individuals might have the same socializing experience as the former state legislators.

SUMMARY

In this chapter, I have tried to ascertain something about the background of members implicated in relational conflict over the years. To make sure the implicated members were truly more uncivil, I used two unique model specifications. First, I consider only members mentioned multiple times in newspaper articles. Second, I use a count of the number of newspaper articles a member appears in. I also suspected that newspaper reporters pay closer attention to congressional leaders and have controlled for this possibility in the modeling. I certainly have not developed a definitive test. However, I believe I have initiated the systematic study of uncivil members of Congress. My hope is that others will find other unique ways to identify uncivil members and perhaps dig a little deeper into their personality traits and backgrounds. For now, I hope I have provided an important starting point.

Since Jeannette Rankin (R-MT) became the first female elected to the House of Representatives in 1916, many other women have served with great distinction. We now know that women, on average, appear less likely to contribute to relational conflict. I would be remiss, however, if I did not make mention of the intraparty battle between the two Republican women, Marjorie Taylor Green (R-GA) and Lauren Boebert (R-CO), in the 118th Congress (2023–2025), that was discussed briefly in chapter 1. These women do not appear in the database. I stopped the systematic collecting of names with the 116th Congress (2019–2021). Given the relatively small sample size of women in Congress, the findings regarding female may not withstand the test of time, especially if the rabble-rousing tendencies of Representatives Green and Boebert are indicative of a new type of female legislator.

I would be equally remiss if I failed to tell more of Rankin's story. For the purpose of this book, her story is an important one. Representative Rankin was among the fifty House members who voted against U.S. entry into World War I. Her opponent used her vote against her in the 1918 election campaign, which she lost. Yet, Rankin remained a public figure and a committed pacifist for the next 20+ years and was re-elected to the House from Montana in the 1940 election cycle. Notably, she was the only House member to vote against a declaration of war on Japan in the aftermath of the attacks on Pearl Harbor. Her story is important for at least two reasons. First, Rankin's commitment to world peace was unquestionable, which is consistent with the findings reported in the chapter that women can contribute to more civility in political discourse. In Rankin's public life, she was certainly steadfast and opinionated, a strong woman one might say, but she also maintained a certain dignity and thoughtfulness in all of her political endeavors (Lopach and Luckowski 2005).

Second, Rankin's story reminds us there are unpopular issue positions that deserve an airing. Rankin accepted ridicule for her vote against war with Japan. However unpopular her position was it was certainly principled. British Prime Minister Neville Chamberlain famously notes, "In war, whichever side may call itself the victor, there are no winners, only losers".[4] The nonviolent commitment of important political leaders such as Dr. Martin Luther King and Mahatma Gandhi, in the mid-twentieth century, also comes to mind. These individuals exemplified the same kind of commitment to peace that the Honorable Representative Rankin maintained throughout her life. A position, which although unpopular, certainly deserves special attention and careful consideration. Her presence in Congress is yet another piece of evidence that one can be principled while maintaining civility and avoiding personal confrontations.

Regarding other findings, preliminarily, it seems that members, who have served in a state or perhaps local legislature, will better understand what it takes to get along with the other members of a democratically elected assembly. Specifically, members of Congress who have served in state legislators for five or more years are clearly less likely to find themselves in public personality battles while serving in the national legislature. This finding is quite robust and withstands multiple measurement strategies. Still more, we now have evidence that throughout a 144-year period of congressional history, members who deviated from their party mean vote position were more likely to appear in newspaper articles as engaging in relational conflict. Contrary to what many imagine, the uncivil members are not, on average, ideologues who contribute disproportionately to party system polarization, instead, they are Party Mavericks who often engage in intraparty disputes and ignore the voting position of party leaders and a majority of the members of their own political party. It bears repeating, as a group, the uncivil ones do not contribute to party system polarization.

Moving this analysis forward, the ramifications of high, medium, and low legislative conflict must receive additional scrutiny. A better understanding of a productive legislature is required. Moreover, I wish to test the relationship between moderate conflict and legislative productivity in multiple ways to ensure, as best as possible, that whatever findings I uncover are not the result of a particular measurement strategy. In this context, in the next chapter, I will discuss an indicator of Topical Legislative Productivity that I have created, and will compare this to alternative indicators of Congress-by-Congress legislative productivity. In this regard, there is considerable scholarship that deserves mention. In the end, I will focus the tests of LCT on my novel measurement strategy. However, in the testing, which appears in chapter 6, as a validity check, I will also test the precepts of LCT using a better-established measure of Congress-specific legislative accomplishment produced by Joshua Clinton and John Lapinski (2006).

NOTES

1. Using calculus, the modeling converts the "0's" and "1's" representing relational conflict to probabilities, then odds, and finally to the logit function or the log of odds. To learn more about this modeling choice, see https://www.ibm.com/topics/logistic-regression (last accessed August 8, 2023).

2. To learn more about this modeling choice, see https://www.sciencedirect.com/topics/psychology/poisson-regression#:~:text=Poisson%20regression%20is%20used%20to,the%20frequency%20of%20an%20event (last accessed August 8, 2023).

3. Editorial, *New York Times*, June 6, 1900, 5.

4. To find this quote, see Oxford Reference at https://www.oxfordreference.com/display/10.1093/acref/9780191826719.001.0001/q-oro-ed4-00002794;jsessionid=052BB4704EAA7C371627A8D0A219D1ED#:~:text=In%20war%2C%20whichever%20side%20may,winners%2C%20but%20all%20are%20losers (last accessed 14 August, 2023).

Chapter 5

Measuring Legislative Productivity

There has been significant scholarly debate about the proper measurement of legislative productivity. Everyone seems to take exception to some facet of existing strategies. The controversy likely exists because there is no such thing as a perfectly valid measure of any concept in the social sciences, not the least of which is an equivocal idea like "productivity." I suggest it would be sensible to accept this fact and instead of looking for reasons one measure is better, simply acknowledge that each is unique and likely capturing some distinctive dimension of the broad concept of productivity. That said, different measures ought to correlate with one another at least to a certain extent. Nearly everyone would agree that the 1930s and the New Deal era, along with the 1960s and the Great Society programs of the Lyndon Johnson administration, represent productive periods of congressional history. If one creates a new measure of legislative productivity, and it suggests the 1940s and 1950s were more productive than the 1930s or 1960s, there was likely a faulty measurement assumption made or perhaps there is a typo in the formula used to derive the decade-specific values.

Sarah Binder (1999; 2003), for her part, makes the case that a simple enumeration of legislative achievements, Congress-by-Congress, is an insufficient indicator of productivity. Her position is that it is necessary to control for the relative demand for new legislation under the assumption that in some periods of congressional history there are issues that are more pressing. In other words, a more attentive public, in certain eras, may create demand for extra legislative action. Morris Fiorina (1992) concurs, on some level, and suggests that divided party control of government commonly occurs in "troubled" times and that there is consequently more demand for legislative action under divided party control of the executive and legislative branches. He concludes that equal amounts of supply under both unified and divided party control indicate that the government's response under divided government is unsatisfactory (Fiorina 1992, 90).

I suggest both Binder and Fiorina offer commendable discernments and scholars should take their insights seriously. To a large degree, their arguments, certainly Binders', is a response to David Mayhew (1991) who uses both contemporaneous and retrospective judgments to count landmark legislative accomplishments, Congress-by-Congress. Many have followed Mayhew's lead and tried to improve on his measurement strategies (Kelly 1993; Edwards III, Barrett, and Peake 1997; Coleman 1999; Howell et al. 2000). Valerie Heitshusen and Garry Young (2006) use the *United States Code* to extend the analysis of landmark legislative productivity back in time. Much of the previous work on productivity, or gridlock, had been limited to a post-World War II analysis and these efforts to extend the timeline are an important contribution (*see also* Brady 1988).[1] Measures with a more limited timeline may miss relevant variation as it relates to structural arrangements such as divided government and presidential honeymoons, but their is also variation in two-dimensional legislative conflict and moderation that one ought to consider. Of course, the extension back in time is of value only when one can be relatively certain that the different Congresses studied are comparable.

Joshua Clinton and John Lapinski (2006; 2007) have developed an impressive and comprehensive approach to measuring legislative productivity across a long historical period. Their work uses twenty elite evaluations of legislative enactments and an item-response model to integrate the information contained in the ratings to establish what they call "Legislative Accomplishment" going back to 1877. In their work, Clinton and Lapinski also use information regarding the amount of time Congress devotes to each statute and whether a conference committee was required, among other considerations, to determine the relative significance of legislation passed. Their work represents a major effort to define meaningful legislative output, but like Mayhew (1991), does not address Binder or Fiorina's concern for the demand for legislation.

I will offer yet another measurement strategy in this chapter. My position is not that I have developed the best or even a better measure of legislative productivity than those I have just cited. The motivation for this new effort is a sincere attempt to address the demand consideration brought forth by Binder and Mayhew in a parsimonious manner while developing a measure that stretches back far enough in time to obtain reasonable tests of LCT and my thesis regarding the value of moderate conflict. I am especially cognizant of the need for a measure that does not mix unlike periods of congressional history. For instance, comparing the pre- and post-Civil War Congresses could be problematic because the current party system did not exist in the antebellum or pre–Civil War period.

MEASURING LEGISLATIVE PRODUCTIVITY
(CONGRESS-BY-CONGRESS)

I base my new measure of legislative productivity on reporting in the *Congressional Digest* (*Digest*), and my analysis extends back to the 67th Congress (1921–1923). I have extended the analysis through the end of the Donald J. Trump administration, in 2020. One can quite easily update the measure, as long as the *Digest* is in continuous publication and editors with the journal do not fundamentally alter their congressional coverage. The *Digest* began publishing in 1921 in response to the women's suffrage movement. A desire to provide nonpartisan policy information to newly enfranchised women voters, after the nineteenth amendment passed, motivated the journal's original editor, Alice Robinson. Beginning my measurement in 1921, holds constant Reed's Rules adopted in the early 1890s and the provision of cloture in the Senate, adopted in 1917. Both changes suggest a more partisan legislative process akin to the one occurring in the 2010s and 2020s.[2]

I hold that it is possible to make the case that in a mass society, like the United States, with considerable economic disparities, and cultural and ethnic diversity, there is always a demand for new legislation. Certainly, each Congress has had a schedule put before it. The legislative program, or agenda, I suggest serves as a proxy for demand. Each biennial Congress faces calls from the attentive public, in the form of policy prescriptions, to address the salient issues of the time. As long as I have been studying politics, for the past 30 years, if someone learns I am a political scientist, my new acquaintance will remark, "Wow, these must be interesting times for you." The quip has been the same for 30 years and I expect it was likely around long before I started studying politics and will be around long after I retire. My position is that any "time" and/or "all times" have been interesting. Certainly, there are always prominent issues placed before Congress. The question then becomes how well Congress handles the agenda put before it. Surely, some Congresses address the topical issues of the day more completely than others do.

What I have developed is a measure of Topical Legislative Productivity. The *Digest* provides the agenda, or topics, and has done so in a consistent fashion for a little over 100 years. Specifically, the *Digest* seeks to identify and discuss what it refers to as "controversial" policy topics in each Congress. To be explicit, I am suggesting this topical agenda represents a demand for legislative action. Using the *Digest* provides me with an independent source to determine the major policy struggles going on in each Congress, and I do not need to develop my own list of important issues based on my judgment about the significant topics each Congress faces. Put differently, I consider the *Digest* topics to represent demand for legislative action, and I wish to learn which topics each Congress ultimately addresses with new public laws.

I concede this may not be the precise type of demand that Binder and Mayhew considered; but nonetheless, it is a type of relevant demand. The measure aims to answer the question, how well does each Congress tackle the controversial agenda put before it?

Importantly, using the *Digest* allows me to extend the analysis of policy productivity across the quarter-century before the post-World War II era, while also including contemporary Congresses. The *Digest* has a reputation for providing nonpartisan policy analysis and doing so in a professional manner, publishing informed analysis and contrasting points of view about each topic it covers, and refraining from partisan or policy endorsements. Its identification of major controversial legislation thus appears balanced and neutral in character, focused on a broad range of issues salient across the two major political parties.

This new measure of productivity also takes into account the "quality" of legislative output. A concern others note is especially important (Mayhew 1991; Kelly 1993). This occurs, largely, because the *Digest* hones in on only a single topic in each issue. There are ten issues of the journal published each year or twenty per Congress. In many Congresses, the *Digest* reserves one issue for post-election coverage and consequently, there are commonly nineteen topics covered in each biennial Congress, although with some variation. The topics covered by the *Digest* change with party control of Congress and the White House. For instance, in the Obama Administration, the *Digest* covered legislative proposals intended to ease tensions between the U.S. and Cuba, discussing a repeal of the Helms-Burton Act, which was the law that codified the embargo on Cuban goods. Earlier in the Obama Administration, one of the topics covered by the *Digest* was The Employment Non-Discrimination Act intended to end discrimination based on gender identity in the workplace. When the president changes, *Digest* coverage changes. The last issue in the 115th Congress (2017–2019) covered Trump Administration attempts to bring back the citizenship question on the U.S. Census, noting the Census used the question from 1890 to 1950. The first issue in the 116th Congress (2019–2021) discusses criminal justice reform, legislation supported by President Trump. Appendix B provides a random listing of the topics covered by the *Digest* (three topics per decade), since the 1920s.

The *Digest* is easily available online and manageable in its size, aiding replication of this study by students and scholars. Importantly, once an individual Congress adjourns *sin die,* it is possible to update the analysis and stay current. For now, I analyze the fifty Congresses from 1921 through 2020. Aiding the comparability of the Congresses in our analysis, each Congress occurs after the seventeenth and nineteenth amendments, which establish the direct election of senators and women's suffrage. Moreover, the size and format of the *Digest* are virtually unchanged across these Congresses. Each issue includes statements by members of Congress, with opposing views on the pending legislative matter. Importantly, the existence of the pro position supports my position that the articles serve as a reasonable proxy for the demand for legislative action.

To calculate a Congress-specific indicator of productivity, I first identify the relevant pending legislative matters as presented in the journal. I then comb the *United States Statutes at Large* to see if there was a public law passed in the concurrent Congress on the topic. I count the law as evidence of topical legislative success if the legislation passed before the Congress in question adjourns *sine die*. It is important to note that in each instance, there is no subjective concern for the ideological content of the specific legislation passed or if the measure passed was "comprehensive." My sole concern is whether there was any law passed that dealt with the specific topic discussed in the *Digest*.[3] In the more modern period, this involved reading the outlines of omnibus spending bills, and I did find some of the new laws in these compilations. For instance, the Trump Administration tax cuts were the subject of the first *Digest* issue in 2018, during the 115th Congress, and I find this legislation in "An Act to Provide for Reconciliation Pursuant to titles II and V of the Concurrent Resolution on the Budget for Fiscal Year 2018," a new law which included many different provisions. Fortunately, congressional leaders treat most topics addressed by the *Digest* as standalone legislative matters. Often, the *Digest* identifies a specific House or Senate bill number in their discussion of the pending legislation.

In all, there are 995 issues of the *Digest* published between October 1921 and December 2020. Unfortunately, some issues are not usable. There are two reasons. As already noted, some issues cover a recent congressional election, while others cover matters related to a new or retiring Congress and do not focus on a primary legislative agenda item. For instance, in 1923, the second issue of the *Digest* focused on the profiles of the members who would serve in the 68th Congress (1923–1925) and the third issue discusses the opening days of the 68th Congress. In all, 58 of the 995 issues are unusable because they do not discuss a singular topic. Besides this consideration, another 26 issues discuss topics that already saw a new law pass before the *Digest* went to press. In effect, the "demand" had been satiated. Arguably, this occurs because the legislation was pending when editors went to work covering the topic, but the law passed before they went to press. These two considerations leave 911 usable issues representing the same number of legislative topics. Of these, 209 topics saw a law passed during the concomitant Congress.

Figure 5.1 presents Congress's specific values of topical legislative productivity calculated as the percentage of topics that saw legislative action and resulted in a new public law. Note in the Figure that three Congresses surpass a 45 percent pass rate. They are the 73rd (1933–1935), the 89th

76 Chapter 5

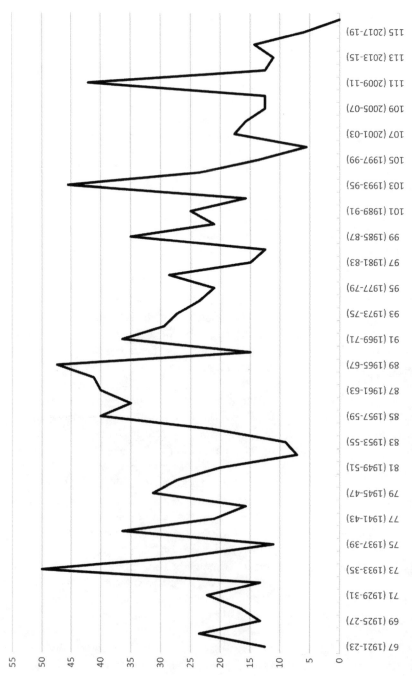

Figure 5.1 Percent of Digest Topics Passed by Concurrent Congress. *Source*: Original data compiled by the author.

(1965–1967), and the 103rd (1993–1995). The first two are likely no surprise to close observers of Congress because they appear at the onset of the New Deal of the Franklin Roosevelt Administration in the 1930s and the Great Society program of the Lyndon Johnson Administration in the 1960s. The third instance is Bill Clinton's honeymoon Congress, which occurs under unified political party control of government. In fact, all three instances are honeymoon Congresses with unified party control of Congress and the White House. The Clinton first Congress saw the passage of the Family and Medical Leave Act of 1993 (P.L. 103–3) and the National Voter Registration Act of 1993 or the "Motor Voter" law (P.L. 103–31). In addition, the first Clinton Congress passed the North American Free Trade Agreement Implementation Act (P.L. 103–182) and the Violent Crime Control and Law Enforcement Act of 1994 (P.L. 103–322), which included an assault weapons ban. The *Digest* gave issue-length coverage to each of these topics prior to their passage.

Note, also, in figure 5.1, that the success of the Clinton Administration is short-lived and topical legislative productivity, after the reestablishment of divided government in the 104th Congress (1995–1997), drops off precipitously. The 106th Congress, Clinton's last, which included a presidential impeachment trial, experiences very low productivity. This is also the case for the 116th Congress (2019–2021), defined in part, by the first impeachment of President Donald J. Trump. The 116th is the low point for productivity in the time series. Congress passed no laws in the 116th addressing the topics covered by the *Digest*. Some of the topics covered included the tightening of food stamp eligibility, attempts to roll back automobile fuel efficiency standards, and legislation to address cannabis-banking concerns.

It bears mentioning that some topics such as a call for the creation of a cabinet level Department of Education appear in multiple issues of the *Digest*. The first issue dedicated to the creation of the new cabinet bureaucracy occurred in December 1921, the second in February 1924, the third in May 1926, and the last in November 1978. Ultimately, Congress creates the Department of Education in October 1979 with Public Law 96–88. The topic mentioned most in the *Digest* is reform of the Electoral College, with eleven different issues covering the subject. The first time was in the March 1941 issue, then the *Digest* covers the topic in June/July 1944, April 1948, August/September 1949, August/September 1953, April 1956, November 1967, January 1970, January 2001, January 2017, and June of 2020. To date, there has been no successful legislative action on the topic.

If a *Digest* issue is published after a Congress has adjourned *sine die* but prior to the next Congress convening, which occurs principally in the early years of this analysis, I count the issue as part of the "demand" for action in the next Congress. For instance, the *Digest* would have published the February 1923 issue before the 68th Congress was sworn in. Nevertheless,

I code it as being an actionable item for the 68th Congress because the 67th Congress had already adjourned *sine die*. In one of the tests of LCT, each relevant topic will be the unit of analysis. In this model run, the dependent variable will be dichotomous, scored "1" if a new statute passes and "0" if no law passes addressing the *Digest* topic in the concurrent Congress. In a few instances, there are multiple laws passed dealing with a particular topic in a single Congress, but I do not give any additional weight to this consideration.

Figure 5.2 provides a breakdown of topical legislative productivity by presidential administration. The most successful president, based on this calculation, is John F. Kennedy and the least successful is Donald J. Trump. There were thirty-two issues of the *Digest* published while Kennedy was president; however, only twenty-eight of the issues addressed a single usable topic. Of these twenty-eight topics, the coexisting Congresses passed new laws addressing twelve of them. Included were the Housing Act of 1961 (P.L. 87–70), the Foreign Assistance Act of 1961 (P.L. 87–195), and the Public Welfare Amendments of 1962 (P.L. 87–543), which included federal aid for depressed areas of the country. The high Kennedy Administration score is not surprising because the 87th Congress (1961–1963) was the first with unified party control since the Truman Administration eight years earlier.

The high score for the 91st Congress (1969–1971) in the Nixon Administration is more surprising perhaps, as this occurs amidst split political party control of government. Among the topics addressed by the 91st Congress are water pollution controls (P.L. 91–439) and cigarette labeling requirements, including restrictions on cigarette advertising (P.L. 91–222). Some forget that in this earlier era these sorts of topics garnered bipartisan support. The lone topic addressed by new legislation in the Trump Administration was the Tax Cuts and Jobs Act of 2017 (P.L. 115–97), which can be found in the omnibus reconciliation bill passed in 2017.

I hold that figures 5.1 and 5.2 present reasonable evidence that the new measure of legislative productivity has merit. No one will likely be surprised that the Hoover and Harding Administrations were less productive than the Nixon and Eisenhower Administrations. However, it is important that the topical legislative productivity indicator relate to existing measures of productivity, at least to a certain extent. It is not the case that different measures should be identical. Methodologies are so distinct that it is not realistic to expect the different measure to correlate at a very high rate (for instance, $r > .90$). However, if there is no correspondence or intersection that would suggest something is amiss with the indicator I am sponsoring.

Table 5.1 compares the topical legislative productivity measure to four existing indicators of Congress-specific productivity. The first comparison is with an indicator I created, with co-author Lawrence Dodd (Dodd and Schraufnagel 2012; Dodd and Schraufnagel 2013a), and is a count of

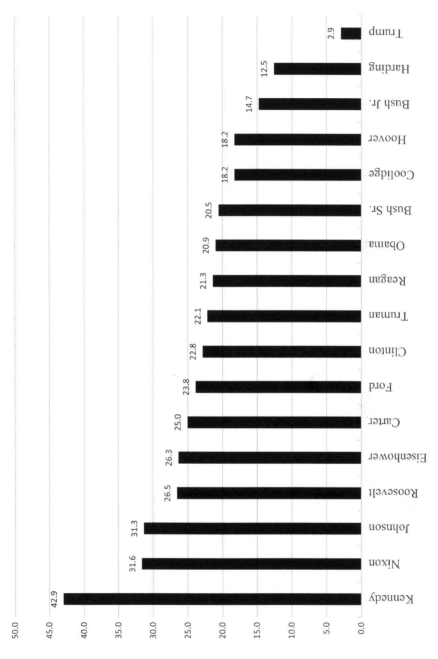

Figure 5.2 **Percent of New Laws that Address Digest Topics: By Presidential Administration.** *Source:* Original data compiled by the author.

Table 5.1 Comparing the *Digest* Indicator of Topical Legislative Productivity to Other Indicators

	Topical Legislative Productivity	Landmark Laws	Binder's Gridlock 2	Binder's Gridlock 4	Legislative Accomplishment
Topical Legislative Productivity	1				
Landmark Laws	.545 *** (n = 37)	1			
Binder's Gridlock 2	-.350 [a] (n = 27)	-.442 * (n = 24)	1		
Binder's Gridlock 4	-.371 [a] (n = 34)	-.469 * (n = 24)	.873 *** (n = 27)	1	
Legislative Accomplishment	.217 (n = 37)	.483 ** (n = 37)	-.111 (n = 24)	-.030 (n = 24)	1

Source: Compiled by author. Gridlock data available as an Appendix in Binder (2003) and I would like to thank Josh Clinton for supplying me with their data.
*** $P < .001$; ** $P < .01$; * $P < .05$; [a] $P < .10$ (two-tailed tests)

Landmark Laws, by Congress, going back to the First Congress (1787–1789) and carried through the 103rd Congress (1993–1995). We label a new public law a "landmark law" if five of fifteen major books or encyclopedias on Congress and American politics, published after 1994, mentioned the enactment.[4] The second and third are indicators of legislative gridlock developed by Sarah Binder (2003). In all, Binder creates five measures of gridlock and I use her *Gridlock 2 and Gridlock 4* indicators for comparison purposes.[5] Because hers are measures of gridlock and not productivity, the expectation is that they will correlate negatively with the other assessments. The fourth is the Clinton and Lapinski (2007) indicator of *Legislative Accomplishment*. Each of the four additional measures has Congress-specific values and table 5.1 compares them to the *Topical Legislative Productivity* indicator, which is simply the percentage of *Digest* topics that the concurrent Congress collared with new laws.

Note straightaway in table 5.1 that the "*n*," or sample size, is different for each correlation test. This occurs because the authors of these measures are looking at different periods of time and the sample size simply equals the number of Congresses where the measures overlap. Considering the Topical Legislative Productivity measure, it correlates in a statistically significant manner with three of the four other measures. The exception is the Clinton and Lapinski indicator of Legislative Accomplishment. Note, however, the correlation is still positive and is nearing statistical significance ($P < .10$; one tailed-test). Binder's Gridlock measures correlate well with both of the measures I have created; however, her measure does not relate well to the Clinton and Lapinski measure. Overall, I suggest, the Topical Legislative Productivity measure holds up reasonably well. The average correlation with the other measures is quite high. The measure of Landmark Laws is also highly correlated with the other indicators, but it is not possible to keep this measure current because it relies on the retrospective judgment of the historical record; hence, its desirability for testing LCT is more limited.

To provide a second test of the two-dimensional conflict-moderation thesis, I will also use the Clinton and Lapinski (2006) data on legislative accomplishment in multivariate testing, which I present in chapter 6. Their measure starts with the 45th Congress (1877–1879), coincidentally, the same starting point as the newspaper measure of relational incivility I have developed and discussed in chapter 2. Although the longer timeline is nice, it does create a scenario where the Congresses tested are more dissimilar in legislative approaches, which might confound matters. Nonetheless, as I indicated earlier, one needs to test theories multiple ways to ensure a specific measurement strategy is not responsible for the results obtained. The *Digest* measure and the Clinton and Lapinski indicator could not be more dissimilar in terms of measurement strategy; yet they relate to one another reasonable well. Given the goal of each is to capture a type of productivity, with Congress-specific values, they should each provide a competent test of LCT.

SUMMARY

This chapter has tackled more prickly measurement issues. It was not long ago that a political scientist might suggest a new theory or idea about what she believes is occurring in Congress and others would simply assess the idea from their own experiences in studying the national legislature. For instance, Fiorina (1992) does not provide any empirical evidence that there is more demand for legislative innovation under divided party control of government. He simply offers a compelling argument. Unfortunately, those opportunities have seemed to slip away. In the contemporary context, fellow political scientists rarely see "force of argument" as sufficient evidence to support a new idea. One must develop measures of the concepts introduced and engage in empirical hypothesis testing. To that end, I have introduced a measure of legislative productivity, which addresses issues of demand for legislation, the quality of legislation, and a measure that is replicable and can reasonably be kept current. Yet, it is likely not enough to rely on a single measure. Hence, I will use another well-established indicator of legislative productivity for testing the precepts of LCT in the next chapter.

Indeed, in all the modeling that I discuss, and ultimately use in chapter 6, I will make a concerted effort to employ multiple measurement strategies of concepts as a means to test the veracity of my findings. I have a decidedly positivist orientation and actually appreciate the scrutiny. For now, I believe, I have developed a reasonably face-valid indicator of a particularly poignant type of legislative productivity. Namely, can Congress handle the agenda that the attentive public, which includes members of Congress, places before it? It is important to realize that the *Digest* is not editorializing. The journal simply uses the topics that members in each Congress have proposed, perhaps by their own volition or because of pressure from organized interests. The concern becomes, can Congress handle its own agenda? My hunch is that the extent to which Congress can will depend on moderation and the interplay of party polarization and relational conflict.

NOTES

1. J. Tobin Grant and Nathan Kelly (2008) try to combine the insights of other scholars and develop indices of congressional productivity. A desire to have indicators of productivity that cover the entire history of Congress motivates their efforts. Yet, their measures have never really caught on among congressional scholars. Especially

disconcerting is that the two measures they create, a Legislative Productivity Index and a Major Legislation Index, take on some radically distinct Congress-specific values. The values on their two indices, both intended to capture some dimension of productivity, are not statistically linked to one another, which is concerning.

2. I should note that my co-author Lawrence Dodd and I have used *Digest* coverage in previous work on legislative productivity (Dodd and Schraufnagel 2009; 2013b; 2017). However, I now have more Congresses to consider, and the intentions have shifted away from a focus on party polarization and divided government to testing LCT. To be clear, I have also studied relational conflict in the past, labeling it "incivilities" in the legislative process (Schraufnagel 2005; Dodd and Schraufnagel 2012). However, the earliest work focuses only on the confirmation of federal judges and justices, and the other the retrospective judgment of Landmark Laws. These earlier works did not consider contemporary topical legislative productivity.

3. I have chronicled all the public law numbers I use to justify a topic resulting in a new law and this data is available upon request.

4. The sources consulted include:

Congressional Histories:

Christianson, Stephen G. 1996. *Facts about the Congress*. New York: The H.W. Wilson Company.

Landsberg, Brian K., ed. 2004. "Timeline." In *Major Acts of Congress: Gale Virtual Reference Library*. 3 Volumes. New York: Macmillan Reference USA.

Remini, Robert V. 2006. *The House: The History of the House of Representatives*. New York: Harper Collins Books.

Stathis, Stephen W. 2003. *Landmark Legislation, 1774–2002: Major U.S. Acts and Treaties*. Washington D.C.: CQ Press.

Congressional Encyclopedias:

Bacon, Donald C., Roger H. Davidson, and Morton Keller, eds. 1995. *The Encyclopedia of the United States Congress*. New York: Simon & Schuster.

DewHirst, Robert E. 2007. *Encyclopedia of the United States Congress*. New York: Facts on Files Inc.

Tarr, David R. and Ann O'Connor, eds. 1999. *Congress A-Z*. 3rd Ed. Washington, D.C.: CQ Press.

Presidential Histories:

Jewell, Elizabeth. 2005. *U.S. Presidents Fact Book*. New York: Random House Reference.

Kane, Joseph Nathan. 1998. *Presidential Fact Book*. New York: Random House, Inc.

Presidential Encyclopedias:

Levy, Leonard W., and Louis Fisher, eds. 1994. *Encyclopedia of the American Presidency*. New York: Simon & Shuster.

Nelson, Michael, ed. 1992. *CQ's Encyclopedia of American Government: The Presidency A to Z*. Washington D.C.: Congressional Quarterly Inc.

American History:

ABC-Clio. 2007. *America: History and Life*.

American History Encyclopedia:

Finkleman, Paul, and Peter Wallenstein. 2001. *The Encyclopedia of American Political History*. Washington D.C.: CQ Press.

Public Policy Encyclopedias:

Jackson, Byron M. 1999. *Encyclopedia of American Public Policy*. Santa Barbara, CA: ABC-Clio Inc.

Rabin, Jack, ed. 2003. *Encyclopedia of Public Administration and Public Policy*. New York: Marcel Dekker, Inc.

5. I obtained very close to the same results regardless of the Binder Gridlock measure employed for comparison.

Chapter 6

Moderate Conflict and Legislative Productivity

Throughout this book, I have discussed policy productivity as involving the success of Congress in enacting new laws. Implicitly, I have suggested that each Congress will be the unit of analysis in empirical testing. Scholars have employed this approach, predominantly thus far, in analyzing productivity (Mayhew 1991; Binder 1999; 2003; Theriault 2008). It will be important that I likewise report findings in this manner to allow readers to compare the results with those of other analysts. I use the percentage of *Congressional Digest* topics addressed by new laws, in each Congress, as the dependent variable when Congress is the unit of analysis.

The drawback of using each Congress as the unit of study is that this foregoes the opportunity to control for considerations such as the amount of time left in a Congress when a topic reaches agenda status. For instance, in Binder's (2003) work that uses *New York Times* (*Times*) editorials to define the issue agenda, it is not clear at what point in the Congress the *Times* was discussing the specific topics used in the analysis. Congressional scholars readily recognize that legislation often fails because time simply runs out in a particular Congress. Similarly, a Congress-by-Congress analysis does not allow one to gauge how much work Congress has done to ready legislation for passage by the time an issue reaches salient or topical status. For instance, it might be that the demand for a new law is relatively new and there has been little previous consideration; in other instances, the demand for action may occur after substantial behind-the-scenes preparation has already taken place. When each Congress is the unit of study, a systematic occurrence of either scenario might confound matters.

To deal with these and other concerns, I develop a second strategy that uses each topic examined by the *Digest* as the unit of analysis. In doing so, I am asking what conditions are likely to produce the enactment of a law on a particular policy topic, in a particular Congress, given the conflict context that defines that Congress. In terms of LCT, a moderately polarized Congress is more likely to pass a law than a Congress that has either too little or too much conflict. This shift in perspective increases the unit of analysis from 50 Congresses, the 67th to the 116th, to the 911 usable topics that the *Digest* discussed across these same Congresses.

Recall from chapter 5, there were 995 issues of the *Digest* between 1921 and the end of 2016. I use only 911 of them in the analysis because 58 issues were dedicated to summaries of presidential or legislative elections or some other non-topic specific coverage, and another 26 issues dealt with a topic after new legislation had already passed the relevant Congress. Calculated in this manner, the number of topics per Congress varies from twelve in the 70th Congress (1927–1929) to 22 in several Congresses. On average, there are 18.2 *Digest* topics per Congress, in the time period analyzed.

In the multivariate testing, I control for several other considerations, which ought to influence topical legislative productivity. When each Congress is the unit of analysis, I use a Prais-Winsten Regression to correct for possible autocorrelation of error terms that can occur as the result of data arrayed over time. When each *Digest* topic is the unit of analysis, I use a Mixed-Effects Logistic Regression. I use a logistic transformation because the dependent variable is dichotomous scored "1" if a *Digest* topic is addressed by a new law in the contemporaneous Congress and "0" otherwise. I need a mixed-effects or hierarchical model because eight different predictors, including the different conflict measures, have only Congress-specific values. Three additional predictors do vary by *Digest* topic. A more complete elaboration of all measurement strategies follows.

As a robustness check, I test LCT and the value of moderate conflict using an entirely different dataset. Specifically, I use the Clinton-Lapinski (2006) measure discussed in chapter 5. Checking back to table 5.1, one notices the indicator of "Legislative Accomplishment," by Congress, is the alternative productivity measure that is least related, or weakly correlated, to the *Digest* measure. My primary motivation for using the Clinton-Lapinski measure is that the data is available for a long enough time that one can get the necessary variation in two-dimensional conflict to gain sufficient contrast for a meaningful test of LCT's moderation thesis. Moreover, the Clinton-Lapinski measure is a well-established indicator. Other researchers have cited their original publication, which appeared in the *American Journal of Political Science* in 2006, over 200 times.

KEY CONFLICT VARIABLES

The most straightforward key explanatory variable is the measure of *Moderate Polarization* explained in chapter 2. Recall, this is an indicator of Senate two-party polarization that has been "folded" so that the median quantity takes on the highest value and lower and higher levels of polarization take on descending values. Specially, I use the quantities displayed in figure 2.4 in chapter 2. Again, I opt for using Senate polarization because of the extra obstructionist opportunities provided by legislative holds, or threats to filibuster, in the Upper Chamber. In addition, I do not average chamber values because roll call votes in the two-chambers, are distinct (Poole and Rosenthal 1997).[1]

It is important to remember that LCT is about more than moderate party polarization. The theory also suggests that legislative conflict is two-dimensional and that relational conflict has additional explanatory power as it relates to legislative productivity. The thesis suggests that a mix of high party polarization and high inter-party relational conflict is particularly troubling for productivity. This is the hyper-conflict that one witnesses in many twenty-first century Congresses and the level of legislative conflict likely to produce gridlock to the point that Congress will be unable to pass even the basic appropriation bills required to keep the government operating. Although Robert Dahl (1967) does not explicitly refer to relational incivilities, this is the "severe" conflict that he theorizes is especially problematic in pluralist democracies.

To capture "severe" conflict, I create a variable equal to *Senate Polarization* multiplied by the percentage of newspaper articles that discuss inter-party relational conflict (*% Inter-Party Relational Conflict*). The product I call *Interactive Two-Dimensional Conflict*. Considering all seventy-two Congresses from 1877 to 2020, the variable produces a high value in the 58th Congress (1903–1905) and a low value in the 83rd Congress (1953–1955). Recall, the 83rd was the Congress with the Army-McCarthy hearings, representing a spike in relational incivilities. However, most of the articles were either intraparty or nonpartisan. Only 10 percent of the relational conflict incidents were inter-party battles. When you consider the 1950s occur when party polarization is arguably too low, the low value of two-dimensional interactive conflict for the 83rd Congress makes sense.

Considering this new measure of interactive two-dimensional conflict, most of the twenty-first century Congresses are in the bottom ten, or the Congresses one must consider the most conflictual in the time period examined. When I use this new consideration in the regression runs, I will need to include the component parts (Senate Polarization and % Inter-party Relational Conflict) in the econometric models. This will provide a more complete test of LCT and the moderation thesis. Specifically, the coefficients and their standard errors obtained from the test of the component parts of the interaction term will also be instructive. For instance, the coefficient obtained for Senate Polarization will be its effect on productivity, in a hypothetical world, where there is no inter-party relational conflict. Correspondingly, the coefficient associated with % Inter-Party Relational Conflict, and its accompanying standard error, will represent a test of inter-party relational conflict on legislative productivity, if there was, hypothetically, no party polarization or voting differences between the two major political parties.

According to LCT, these hypotheticals represent a legislature with too little conflict and the presence of either polarization or inter-party relational conflict ought to increase productivity, all else being equal. The product of the two conflict considerations should relate negatively to productivity. Fortunately, I will be able to test these contentions in three unique ways. First, using Congress as the unit of analysis and the *Digest* measure of topical productivity. Second, using each *Digest* issues as the unit of analysis and third, using the Clinton-Lapinski measure of legislative accomplishment.

CONTROL VARIABLES: CONGRESS AS THE UNIT OF ANALYSIS

To gain a thorough or more complete test of LCT and the conflict indicators just elaborated, it is necessary to account for other considerations that may systematically relate to legislative productivity. My first control variable taps a *Presidential Honeymoon Congress*. The idea is that when we first elect a new president, the attendant Congress will provide the new chief executive some preference and allow them to implement or pass items on their campaign agenda. Consequently, these Congresses ought to be more productive, on average. Given that the president's party will often lose seats, in Congress, in the subsequent mid-term election, it is even more likely that the president's first Congress will be more productive than their second.

The honeymoon concept would seem to be a straightforward consideration and one easy to measure. Simply create a dummy variable scored "1" for the first Congress of a president's term and "0" otherwise. Unfortunately, there are at least two confounding considerations. First, when a president serves for eight years do they get a second honeymoon? One after each election victory? Second, what about a president who takes over for a deceased or resigning president. Is their first Congress a honeymoon, even though they did not win an election campaign?

I answer these questions by relying, in large part, on the insights of Keith Krehbiel (1998, Chapter 3) who argues that the reason honeymoons may be more productive is that the veto pivot changes when there is a new person in the White House. In Krehbiel's view, and in a practical manner he is correct, the only way new laws pass is if the president agrees or if two-thirds of both the House of Representatives and Senate can override the president's veto. If we assume that a president's policy preferences are static, or in Krehbiel's terms, "the president's ideal point is presumed to be fixed" (1998, 61) a honeymoon should occur only when there is a new person in the White House. Corresponding to Krehbiel's insights and considering the first question, I score a Congress "1" only if it is the president's first Congress, following their first election victory. For instance, I score President Bill Clinton's first Congress, the 103rd (1993–1995), "1" but not the 105th (1997–1999), even though he had won re-election in 1996.

Considering the second question, three presidents died in office, and one resigned the office mid-term during the period I am studying. The first instance is the 47th Congress (1881–1883) and I score the Congress "1" because James A. Garfield was a newly elected president when the 47th Congress began. However, he is shot and killed during his honeymoon Congress and Chester A. Arthur, another new president, replaces him. There was a new president in office for the entire 47th Congress and consequently the score of "1", for this Congress, is arguably appropriate. In each of the other three instances, William McKinley, John F. Kennedy, and Richard M. Nixon, the president was replaced during their second Congress and each had already had their "honeymoon" Congress. In the 57th (1901–1903), the 88th (1963–1965) and the 93rd (1973–1975), a new man appears in the White House (T. Roosevelt, L. Johnson, and Ford) mid-Congress. Hence, I score the Congresses .75, .5294, .1818, respectively, representing the proportion of time left before the Congress would adjourn *sine die*, when the new man took over. When Theodore Roosevelt and Lyndon Johnson subsequently win their first election to the country's highest office (the 58th and 89th Congresses), I also score those as presidential honeymoon Congresses.

Consistent with existing research, I expect the honeymoon variable to be positively associated with productivity (Mayhew 1991; Edwards III, Barrett, and Peake 1997; Coleman 1999). As is often the case with social science research, I was tempted and did test other measurement strategies for the honeymoon consideration. Regardless of how I measure the concept, the statistical significance is not particularly strong in fully specified models. In a simple bivariate test and using the fifty Congresses, which have the *Digest* measure of Topical Legislative Productivity available, there is a statistically significant relationship ($r = .34$; $P < .02$; $n = 50$). However, considering the fifty-nine Congresses where I have the Clinton-Lapinski measure of productivity (45th—103rd Congresses), regardless of the measurement strategy, there is no statistically significant bivariate relationship between the honeymoon variable and the productivity measure. Hence, the variation in the statistical significance of the honeymoon consideration seems to be more a product of the measurement of productivity, or the period analyzed, than it is the honeymoon measurement strategy.[2]

Next, I control for *Unified Government* or Congresses when the same political party has their candidate in the White House and majority control of both the Senate and the House of Representatives. Notably, the effect of this consideration on legislative productivity is still unsettled. Krehbiel (1998) offers considerable insight into why there may *not* be a difference between unified and divided party control of government. Specifically, his thesis recognizes the super majoritarian aspects of lawmaking in the United States, which embolden the minority political party, and allows for obstruction in most Congresses, even under unified party control of the government.

David Mayhew (1991) may have initiated the debate surrounding the productivity of unified versus divided party control of government. In his book, *Divided We Govern*, he finds that divided control, on average, can be as productive as unified party control. Still, considerable work, post-Mayhew, has suggested that unified government is more productive (Coleman 1999; Edwards III, Barrett, and Peake 1997; Binder 2003). Again, I suspect the discrepancies have as much to do with the unique dimension of legislative productivity scholars are measuring, along with the possibility that the period studied will affect things. For instance, considering J. Grant and Nathan Kelly's (2008) two measures of productivity and sixty-nine Congresses, from the 45th (1877–1879) to the 108th (2003–2005), one obtains very different relationships between productivity and unified government. Their Major Legislative Index correlates negatively with unified government ($r = -.12$; $P < .37$; $n = 64$) and their broader Legislative Productivity Index correlates positively with unified party control ($r = .12$; $P < .35$; $n = 64$).

In the testing, which follows, I will consider government unified only when the same political party as the president controls both chambers of Congress. I will provide some post hoc consideration of the relationship between split political party control of the two chambers of Congress, or what Sarah Binder (2003, 74–75) has called "quasi-divided" government, and productivity in this chapter's summary. Given the precepts of LCT, I suspect one can consider divided government, or the opposite of unified party government, another conflict variable. Hence, split or unified party control of government may have distinct effects on productivity in polarized and depolarized settings. I am mindful of the possibility that once I account for the moderate or interactive conflict considerations, the statistical link between the *Digest* measure of productivity and Unified Government may be "washed out." Overall, I expect to uphold the null hypothesis of no relationship between one party control of government and legislative productivity.

Third, I consider the legislative capacity of the majority party in the Senate. Specifically, I use an indicator of *Senate Majority Size*, which is equal to the percentage of seats held by the majority party in the Senate at the beginning of a new Congress. Because the minority party in the Upper Chamber is better equipped with obstructionist tools (Sinclair 2006), and because the pivotal legislator is more likely to come from the minority party in the Senate (Krehbiel 1998), I suspect that the size of the majority in the Senate will be especially relevant. Notably, I find a positive bivariate relationship between Senate Majority Size and both the *Digest* and Clinton-Lapinski measures of productivity. Moreover, these relationships are statistically significant or very near significant. For the *Digest* indicator, the association is easily linked ($r = .36$; $P < .02$; $n = 50$) and for the Clinton-Lapinski, it is very close to reaching statistical significance ($r = .22$; $P < .10$; $n = 59$).[3]

Next, a common control variable is some indicator of public mood, which scholars believe can spur a more activist national government (Stimson 1991). David Mayhew (1991) used a dummy variable to measure the public's commitment to activist government, which he scored "1" from 1961–1976. However, John Coleman argues for the Stimson measure (1999, 825), which uses survey data and factor analysis to obtain quarterly, annual, and biennial "public mood" scores. To his great credit, Stimson has kept the public mood variable current. Unfortunately, the Stimson measure goes back only to the 82nd Congress (1951–1953). This reduces the Congress-by-Congress analysis by 15 and prevents a test of the pre-World War II era and the pre-Franklin D. Roosevelt (FDR) Administration Congresses.[4] With some important exceptions, a steady increase in conflict in Congress largely defines the postwar era. The primary motivation for using the *Digest* and Clinton-Lapinski measures of productivity is to stretch back in time to gain more meaningful overtime variation in legislative conflict. To capture "public mood" or a more activist national government, I opt for a simple dummy variable scored "1" for the 73rd Congress (1933–1935) forward. Many observers of American government recognize that since the FDR Administration, the national government has become much more "active" (Kennedy 2009, 253–54; Milkis 2014). I label the variable *Post-New Deal* and anticipate a positive association with the productivity measures.

Whether I use each Congress as the unit of analysis or *Digest* topics, I control for two final considerations, both dummy variables representing a single Congress. The first I call the *Great Depression* (the 73rd Congress-1933–1935) and the second the *Great Recession* (the 112th Congress-2009–2011). The Great Recession consideration falls out in the testing that uses the Clinton-Lapinski measure of productivity because their data stops with the 103rd Congress (1993–1995). These two dummy variables also, arguably, relate to the Stimson (1991) public mood consideration. When great economic hardship befalls a country, the public is likely in the mood for government action. Theda Skocpol and Lawrence Jacobs (2011) provide a treatise on the similarities between the start of FDR and Obama Administrations and by extension the two Congresses I am signaling out. Economic downturns can have a sobering effect on society. Members of Congress must show resolve and move to address the suffering of their constituents. I argue that with the 73rd and 102nd Congresses, the mood had changed, and elected representatives were compelled to act. Correspondingly, I expect a positive and statistically significant association between each variable and the productivity considerations.

CONTROL VARIABLES: *DIGEST* TOPICS AS THE UNIT OF ANALYSIS

When each *Digest* topic becomes the unit of analysis, I use the same set of variables, spelled out and repeat these values for each *Digest* topic in the specific Congress I am considering. This repetition of the values is what causes me to use a hierarchical model, which can account for data that falls into hierarchical or completely nested levels.[5] There is either seven or nine variables with repeated values, considering the two distinct tests of LCT. In the first instance, I am simply testing Moderate Polarization and the six control variables. In the second instance, which uses the interaction term, I have three conflict considerations (Senate Polarization, % Inter-party Relational Conflict, and Interactive Two-Dimensional Conflict) and the six control variables.

Beyond the conflict considerations and control variables already elaborated, I control for three topic-specific considerations. First, because the *Digest* publishes its articles on policy topics throughout a Congress, I control for *Time left* (in months) in the Congress when the *Digest* issue was published. With more time left in the Congress, I expect a greater probability that legislation will pass, and correspondingly, I expect a positive coefficient obtained from the regression run. Additionally, analyzing productivity topic-by-topic allows me to assess how mature different legislative initiatives are. The *Digest* (or any source used to determine demand) may discuss some policy topics after considerable effort to address them has already occurred, whereas other topics may be newer concerns. To control for this, I opt for a simple, yet practical and reliable strategy. I create two dummy variables (*Passed House* and *Passed Senate*) that tap whether any legislation dealing with the topic may have passed one or the other chamber in the extant Congress at the time the *Digest* issue went to press. Although passing a single chamber does not make a law, one must expect a stronger probability of law passage when this has occurred. Of the 911 *Digest* topics used, 187 had already seen new legislation passed in the House at the time of publication, and 124 had seen new legislation passed in the Senate when the issue came out. To sum up, in the topic-by-topic analysis, I add the three topic-specific control variables: *Time Left*, *Passed House*, and *Passed Senate* and always expect a positive association.

RESULTS

Considering the data I have been discussing, there are many ways to test the precepts of LCT. Ultimately, I will need to present the results of the full multivariate regression runs. However, it can be instructive to start with bivariate tests. For instance, simple bivariate tests can expose insights that might be lost if one jumps into more fully specified models. In all, I have four indicators of legislative conflict to consider (Moderate Senate Polarization, Senate Polarization (unfolded), % Inter-Party Relational Conflict, and % Intraparty Relational Conflict) and two measures of productivity (Topical Legislative Productivity and Legislative Accomplishment). Senate Moderation and % Intraparty Relational Conflict should correlate positively with the *Digest Topics* and the *Clinton-Lapinski* measures of productivity. I base this expectation on the hunch that intraparty dissensus will produce crosscutting cleavages and bipartisanship sufficient to move legislation forward. Relatedly, Senate polarization and % Inter-Party Relational Conflict should produce negative coefficients in the bivariate tests of productivity.[6]

Table 6.1 displays the results of the bivariate tests. I list the four conflict indicators first and the two productivity measures at the bottom of the table. Note, in the bottom right-hand corner, there is no statistically significant link between the two productivity measures. There are thirty-seven Congresses where the two productivity indicators overlap. This finding, alone, suggests that any subsequent test of LCT is going to be a strenuous one. It is not the case that I am testing the theory using two nearly identical measures of productivity. Staying in the bottom right corner of the Table, notice that both indicators of productivity produce statistically significant positive correlations with intraparty relational conflict and significant negative correlations with inter-party relational conflict. These are not mirror images of one another because nearly 14 percent of the newspaper articles discuss incivility or relational conflict that is "nonpartisan" or without any obvious partisan context.

Note in the bottom left-hand corner of table 6.1 that the two types of productivity correlate positively with Moderate Polarization, although the Clinton-Lapinski relationship does not reach a standard acceptable level of statistical significance. Of course, we do not know, yet, what will happen in a more fully specified model, which holds other considerations constant. As

Table 6.1 Bivariate Relationships between Legislative Conflict and Legislative Productivity

	Moderate Polarization	Senate Polarization	% Inter-Party Relational Conflict	% Intraparty Relational Conflict	Digest Topics	Clinton-Lapinski
Moderate Polarization	1					
Senate Polarization	.20; P < .10 n = 72	1				
% Inter-Party Relational Conflict	.29; P < .02 n = 72	.49; P < .01 n = 72	1			
% Intraparty Relational Conflict	-.23; P < .06 n = 72	-.21; P < .40 n = 72	-.79; P < .01 n = 72	1		
Digest Topics	.39; P < .01 n = 50	-.40; P < .01 n = 50	-.29; P < .04 n = 50	.28; P < .05 n = 50	1	
Clinton-Lapinski	.17; P < .20 n = 59	-.47; P < .01 n = 59	-.42; P < .01 n = 59	.28; P < .04 n = 59	.22; P < .20 n = 37	1

Source: Compiled by the author, polarization data available at voteview.com, voteview.com/data (last accessed January 15, 2024). Clinton-Lapinski measure provided by Josh Clinton.

Note: A P-value less than .05 represent a conventional indicator of statistical significance. I use two-tailed tests of statistical significance for all of the bivariate analyses reported in this book.

expected, there is a negative correlation between Senate polarization and both indicators of productivity. Note in the top left-hand corner there is a positive correlation between Moderate Polarization and Senate Polarization, although this is not a statistically significant relationship. This occurs because all the polarization values, by Congress, below the median value ($n = 36$) are used as the indicator of moderation. The values of the polarization indicator above the median value ($n = 35$) are folded and the two indicators of Senate conflict diverge from one another at that point.

TOPICAL LEGISLATIVE PRODUCTIVITY AND INTERACTIVE TWO-DIMENSIONAL CONFLICT BY DECADE

Before presenting the results of the tests of LCT that use each Congress and each *Digest* topic as a unit of analysis it should prove interesting to check the relationship between total conflict (Total Newspaper Articles * Senate Polarization) and the *Digest* measure of Topical Legislative Productivity by decade. To be clear this is not the precise indicator of conflict used in the regression runs. Instead it simply represents another operationalization of moderate conflict with considerable face validity. In earlier chapters, I have made the case that any measure of productivity ought to have higher values in the 1930s New Deal Congresses and the 1960s Great Society Congresses, higher especially than the 1940s and 1950s when the Conservative Coalition of Southern Democrats and "lily white" Republicans were able to preserve policies protecting white privilege and the existing economic order. We already know from chapter 5 that the *Digest* measure passes this test, but we do not know if the 1930s and 1960s experience more moderate two-dimensional interactive conflict. I create figure 6.1 to examine the relationship between the topical productivity indicator and an indicator of two-dimensional moderate conflict.[7]

Considering figure 6.1, the decade with the the lowest level of productivity and most conflict is the last one, the 2010s. This decade includes the 112th (2011–2013) through the 116th (2019–2021) Congresses. Note also the convex shape of legislative productivity (Percent Passed) and the concave shape of Total Conflict. This is consistent with LCT and my moderation thesis. When conflict has been the highest in the 1920s, 1990s, 2000s, and 2010s, productivity has been lower. However, notice also that the low levels of conflict in the 1940s and 1950s are likewise not as productive. Representing somewhat of an outlier, the 1970s have very low conflict and this decade is slightly more productive. Yet, the real story is the 1930s and 1960s. These two decades are the most productive and the level of conflict is neither

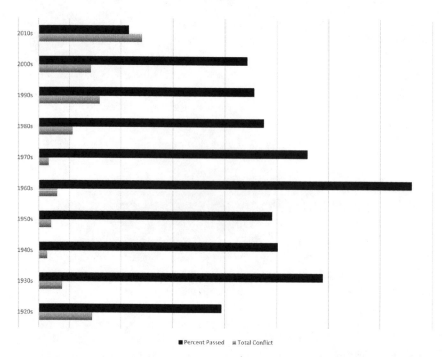

Figure 6.1 Testing Legislative Conflict Theory: Topical Legislative Productivity and Interactive Two-Dimensional Conflict by Decade. *Source*: Original data compiled by the author.

extremely high nor low, consistent with the moderation thesis first discussed in chapter 1. In the next section, I will present tests of LCT that are arguably more complete. For now, this first broad swath analysis suggests the thesis has a reasonable chance of holding up.

Multivariate Tests: Moderate Conflict and Legislative Productivity

The first test uses each Congress as the unit of analysis, the *Digest* measure of topical legislative productivity, and a straightforward test of the moderation thesis. Model A in table 6.2 represents this test. To reiterate, there is only one conflict measure in the equation along with the six control variables. The second test (Model B in the same table) uses the same fifty Congresses (67th–116th) and the interaction of Senate Polarization and % Inter-Party Relational Conflict. In the table(s), I will use an asterisk (*) to indicate a statistically significant relationship.[8] Note straightaway, all the conflict variables are performing as hypothesized. The coefficient in Model A is equal to 73.09 and is more than 2.5 times its standard error. When a coefficient is double the

Table 6.2 Moderate Legislative Conflict and Topical Legislative Productivity

	Model A Coefficient (Standard Error)	Model B Coefficient (Standard Error)
Model: Prais-Winston Regression—Digest Measure of Legislative Productivity		
Conflict Variables		
Moderate Polarization	73.09 * (26.25)	
Senate Polarization		101.60 * (50.80)
% Inter-Party Relational Conflict		1.47 * (.51)
Interactive Two-Dimensional Conflict		-2.52 * (.85)
Control Variables		
Presidential Honeymoon Congress	6.27 * (3.04)	7.39 * (3.02)
Unified Government	-1.13 (3.53)	-3.00 (3.43)
Senate Majority Size	.47 * (.26)	.46 * (.26)
Post-New Deal	5.78 (4.87)	8.46 (5.15)
Great Depression Congress	21.04 * (9.74)	19.99 * (9.20)
Great Recession Congress	18.57 * 9.73	26.22 * (9.98)
Constant	-49.86 * (18.25)	-68.78 * (36.22)
F-Statistic	5.00 *	5.44 *
Adjusted R^2	.36	.45
Sample Size	50	50
d-Statistic (transformed)[5]	1.96	1.98

Source: Compiled by the author.
* Statistically significant at the conventional 95 percent confidence interval (One-tailed test).

standard error, that is an indicator that the relationship is meeting standard levels of statistical significance.

Interpreting the coefficient (73.09) is straightforward. This is the predicted increase in the percentage of *Digest* topics, on average, all else being equal, that is associated with a one-unit increase in moderation. The moderation variable only ranges from approximately .35 to .60 or a difference of .25. Hence, we would expect about an 18 percent increase (73.09 * .25) in *Digest* topics covered by new laws as we move from the most immoderate Congress (116th, 2019–2021) to the most moderate Congress (94th, 1975–1977).

Another way to think of this is in terms of a one standard deviation increase in moderation, which equals approximately .06. A one standard deviation increase in moderation, on average, will be associated with over a four percent increase (73 * .06) in the percentage of *Digest* topics addressed by new laws.

Staying with Model A, notice the presidential honeymoon and Senate majority size considerations are performing as hypothesized. Honeymoons associate with an average increase in productivity of about six percent (6.27 percent). The coefficient of .47, for Senate Majority Size, represents the effect on productivity associated with a one percent increase in the size of the majority party. Given the current 100 member Senate, if the majority party were to gain five seats one might predict more than a two percent (5 * .47) increase in the value of the productivity indicator, on average. The post-New Deal era of activist government does not associate with an increase in productivity once I account for other considerations in the modeling. This is also the case for unified party control of government. In both Model A and B, the Great Depression and Great Recession Congresses associate with about a 20 percent increase in productivity, all else being equal.

Considering Model B, in table 6.2, I now provide a unique test of the moderation thesis. Now I am testing Senate Polarization (not moderation) in conjunction with inter-party relational conflict. I am especially interested in learning what occurs under the hypothetical scenarios of no Senate polarization and no inter-party relational conflict or norm-breaking incivilities. Considering the three conflict variables in Model B, all relate to productivity in the hypothesized manner. Most directly, when Senate polarization and inter-relational conflict increase in tandem we must anticipate more gridlock. The effect is quite large. Specifically, a one standard deviation increase in two-dimensional conflict (17.74) associates with about a 44 percent decrease (17.74 * -2.52) in the percentage of *Digest* topics covered by a new public law.

However, and perhaps more intriguing, are findings associated with the hypothetical scenarios of no Senate polarization and/or no inter-party relational conflict. Results from Model B suggest that more Senate polarization, consistent with the Responsible Party Government thesis (American Political Science Association 1950), would lead to more productivity if there were no inter-party incivilities. Now, members are behaving themselves and not antagonizing the partisan opposition. They are simply voting in a distinct manner from the other party. Distinctive party voting is one of the precepts of Responsible Party Government (American Political Science Association 1950) and if there is no inter-party relational conflict, polarization in a two-party dominant system, with ready-made majorities, equates to more productivity.

It is more difficult to imagine no Senate polarization, yet this is the collusion scenario, I have talked about in authoritarian settings. In the case of the U.S., bipartisan majorities would protect the status quo policies, stifle legislative action, and ignore pressing societal problems. Based on the results displayed in Model B, under this scenario, an increase in inter-party relational conflict ought to break the stalemate and prompt legislative productivity. I will forego an interpretation of the coefficients presented in table 6.2 for these two variables, given they do not represent real-world scenarios. However, the tests do provide considerable affirmation of the precepts of LCT. Namely, absent one or the other type of legislative conflict, an increase in the second dimension of conflict associates with more productivity, all other things being equal. The control variables in Model B perform the same as they did in Model A.

Note on the Prais-Winsten estimation in econometric modeling. The Prais-Winsten estimation is a procedure meant to take care of the serial correlation of autoregressive errors (AR-1). The process transforms the residuals or errors by recursively estimating the coefficients for the variables included in the model, along with the error autocorrelation of a specified model, until reaching sufficient convergence of the AR-1 coefficient. One then obtains estimates using Ordinary Least Squares Regression. Post-estimation, I use a Durbin-Watson d-statistic test to detect if there remains any autocorrelation at lag one in the prediction errors from the regression run. I report the d-statistic in tables 6.2 and 6.3 at the bottom of the tables. D-statistic values range from 0 to 4 and a value around "2" suggests that autocorrelation of the residuals has been accounted for and there is no longer serial correlation of the error terms creating possible bias in the statistical tests.

Clinton-Lapinski Measure of Legislative Accomplishment

Turning to table 6.3, I run the same tests using the Clinton-Lapinski measure of Legislative Accomplishment. Because initial model runs return tests with highly correlated residuals or errors, I include a lag of the dependent variable in the models.[9] Note, I find the same exact relationship between the conflict variables and this wholly distinct indicator of legislative productivity. Notably, the modeling uses a different set of Congresses (46th through the 103rd) to test LCT. One might ask what about the other measures of legislative productivity discussed in chapter 5. Does it work with all of them? The answer is "sort of." Using the number of Landmark Laws based on reporting in encyclopedias, which I created with Lawrence Dodd, the moderation thesis holds using the same set of Congresses as the Clinton-Lapinski measure. In fact, I find the Moderate Polarization variable more strongly linked to productivity. I do not focus on this alternative measure of productivity because my determination of Landmark Laws is retrospective, and I cannot keep the

Table 6.3 Moderate Legislative Conflict and Legislative Accomplishment

Model: Prais-Winsten Regression—Clinton-Lapinski Measure of Legislative Productivity

Conflict Variables	Model C Coefficient (Standard Error)	Model D Coefficient (Standard Error)
Moderate Polarization	.68 * (.28)	
Senate Polarization		.57 * (.34)
% Inter-Party Relational Conflict		.006 * (.003)
Interactive Two-Dimensional Conflict		-.011 * (.005)
Control Variables		
Presidential Honeymoon Congress	.006 (.020)	.002 (.024)
Unified Government	-.009 (.026)	-.015 (.027)
Senate Majority Size	.002 (.002)	.001 (.002)
Post-New Deal	.10 * (.04)	.045 (.044)
Great Depression Congress	.08 (.07)	.106 (.075)
Constant	-1.91 * (.34)	-1.24 * (.30)
F-Statistic	11.79 *	6.86 *
Adjusted R²	.57	.48
Sample Size	58	58
d-Statistic (transformed)[5]	1.92	1.99

Source: Compiled by the author.
* Statistically significant at the conventional 95 percent confidence interval (One-tailed test).

measure current. Considering the Binder (2003) indicator, which is available for only post-World War II Congresses, the moderation thesis does not hold up. This is not overly discouraging. LCT is about important variation in two-dimensional conflict over time. The more limited number of Congresses available for the Binder indicators of gridlock ($n = 27$), I believe, prevents a competent test of LCT.

Congressional Digest Topics as the Unit of Analysis

Next, I test the precepts of LCT using each *Digest* topic as the unit of analysis. I can do this, again, in two different ways. First, simply fold Senate polarization values and create a straightforward indicator of moderate polarization. Second, and more completely, create an interaction between Senate polarization and inter-party relational conflict. It is important to note that I would get a mirror image of the results if I use an interaction between the polarization indicator and the percentage of newspaper articles that are intraparty and nonpartisan combined. I report the results of the topic-specific analysis, with a sample size of 911, covering exactly a 100-year period of congressional history in Models E and F in table 6.4. A close examination of this important test of LCT returns coefficients for the conflict variables all in the hypothesized correct direction. Notably, with the increase in sample size, in the first model (Model E), I find six of the ten explanatory variables statistically linked to productivity in the hypothesized correct direction, and in Model F; eight of twelve variables are statistically linked to productivity. Most importantly, there is a statistically significant tie between each of the conflict variables and topical legislative productivity in the precise manner hypothesized.

Considering the three topic-specific control variables, as expected, these are each important predictors of legislative productivity. The amount of time left in a Congress matters for productivity, as does the maturity of the legislative initiative. When there are more months left before Congress adjourns *sine die,* there is a greater probability of bill passage. This is also the case if related legislation has already passed either the House or the Senate. One should not discount these important control variables, representing the key concepts of time and the maturity of a particular legislative initiative. Yet, these considerations do not explain all the variation in productivity occurring. The conflict variables still matter as well.

Unfortunately, the coefficients reported in the Table are not easy to interpret. To gain some sense of the substantive significance, it is helpful to convert the logit coefficients back to predicted probabilities and then percentages. Considering the base model (Model E), one can note an approximate 12 percent increase in the likelihood of a new law passing as one moves from the most immoderate Congresses to the most moderate, on average, with all the other variables being held constant at either their modal value (dichotomous variables) or mean value (ratio variables). In other words, there is about a .06 probability of a new law addressing the *Digest* topic in the most immoderate Congress (116th, 2019–2021) and this grows to a .18 probability in the most moderate Congress (72nd, 1931–1933), holding other considerations constant as described.

Considering Model F, and the interaction of polarization inter-party relational conflict, as one moves from the most conflictual to the least conflictual scenario, there is a corresponding decrease in the likelihood of a new law of about 93 percent, under the same scenario for control variables described in the previous paragraph. Put differently, there is almost no chance of a new law (.0003

Table 6.4 Moderate Legislative Conflict and Topical Legislative Productivity: Each *Digest* Topic as the Unit of Analysis

	Model: Random Effects Logistical Regression: Congress as the Group Variable	
Conflict Variables	Model E Coefficient (Standard Error)	Model F Coefficient (Standard Error)
Moderate Polarization	4.77 * (1.69)	
Senate Polarization		6.83 * (3.34)
% Inter-Party Relational Conflict		.11 * (.03)
Interactive Two-Dimensional Conflict		-.19 * (.06)
Control Variables		
Presidential Honeymoon Congress	.26 (.18)	.20 (.20)
Unified Government	.11 (.21)	.02 (.21)
Senate Majority Size	.03 * (.01)	.02 (.015)
Post-New Deal	.22 (.30)	.43 (.36)
Great Depression Congress	.98 * (.53)	.96 * (.54)
Great Recession Congress	.70 (.51)	1.67 * (.61)
Topic Specific Control Variables		
Time Left	.04 * (.01)	.04 * (.01)
Passed House	.48 * (.21)	.61 * (.21)
Passed Senate	.50 * (.24)	.58 * (.24)
Constant	-6.76 * (1.15)	-7.29 * (2.37)
Wald Chi²	51.55 *	59.40 *
Number of Groups	50	50
Average Observation per Group	18.2	18.2
Sample Size	911	911

Source: Compiled by the author.
* Statistically significant at the conventional 95 percent confidence interval (One-tailed test).

probability) in the most conflictual scenario, and there is about a 93 percent chance that Congress will pass a new public law that addresses the *Digest* topic when two-dimensional interactive conflict is lowest. Recall, this finding is holding constant both Senate Polarization and % Inter-Party Relational Conflict.

Last, considering the Congress-specific control variables in Models E and F, I get incomplete evidence regarding the honeymoon and unified party government considerations. After controlling for the nature of legislative conflict, the honeymoon and unified government considerations do return positive coefficients, but these are not close to being statistically significant, with the exception of the honeymoon consideration in Model E. The "public mood" considerations perform a little better. Although the Post-New Deal consideration does not produce a statistically significant association, both the start of the Great Depression and the Great Recession are linked to more productivity as hypothesized.

SUMMARY

This chapter has provided six unique tests of LCT and everything holds. Straightforward tests of moderate party polarization and three unique measures of legislative productivity all corroborate the precepts of LCT (Models A, C, and E). Specifically, the results suggest moderate polarization associates with more Topical Legislative Productivity (measured two ways) and more Legislative Accomplishment than either too little or too much distinct party roll call behavior. Arguably, the more complete test of LCT, which uses the interaction term (Models B, D, and F), if also confirming. If there were no relational conflict, more party polarization would lead to more productivity. Similarly, if the political parties were completely undisciplined and there was little or no party system polarization, then, inter-party relational conflict would produce greater legislative accomplishment. Of course, high levels of both types of conflict, working in tandem, as occurs in the second and third decades of the twenty-first century, lead to legislative gridlock.

In this summary, I would like to say more about a couple of the key control variables: Presidential Honeymoon Congresses and Unified Government. First, considering honeymoons and the six distinct model runs, I do find the tests always return a positive coefficient. Moreover, in Models A and B presidential honeymoons are statistically linked to more productivity. However, as I have been suggesting, the honeymoon consideration is somewhat sensitive to the type of productivity one is considering and the time-period analyzed. Keith Krehbiel's (1998) Pivotal Politics Theory suggests honeymoon Congresses might be more productive if the preferences of the legislator who sits at the veto pivot shifts with a new person in the White House. Importantly, the shift will depend on who the new president is and the corresponding new class of legislators. This will affect the veto pivot and the "gridlock interval" may get smaller (more productivity) or larger (less productive). A larger gridlock interval would occur if the new presidents" preferences were more distinct from the two-thirds pivotal legislator rather than less distinct. This would explain why sometimes the honeymoon variable works and other times it does not.

The value of Krehbiel's insight is important. However, I hold it is reasonable to imagine that the honeymoon period may also alter the nature of two-dimensional conflict, and this could likewise explain why some presidents have a honeymoon and others do not. In other words, a honeymoon Congress, in certain eras, might reduce the level of conflict and move things toward more moderation. However, if a contested presidential election produces a new president whom many despise, conflict may not moderate. Correspondingly, the popularity of the new president, and perhaps the size of the election victory, could also explain why some honeymoon Congresses are more productive. A popular president with a significant electoral mandate may cause members of Congress to show deference, at least temporarily, and drop their confrontational style in a manner that moderates conflict in the first session following the national election.

I must also concede that in some ways I have "stacked the deck" against the honeymoon variable in these analyses. My markers for the Great Depression and the Great Recession were both honeymoon Congresses. We learn that the 73rd Congress (1933–1935) and the 111th Congress (2009–2011) were quite productive, and I use these Congresses as proxies for public demand for government action. Action in the face of dire macro-economic conditions. Overall, I suggest that there is not enough evidence in these six tests to discredit the notion that the national legislature will be more productive in a president's first two years in office. Instead, the evidence suggests this could very well be the case.

Considering unified versus divided party control of government, the results reported in this chapter confirm David Mayhew's (1991) insights that when it comes to legislative productivity, unified versus divided government really does not matter. I was somewhat hopeful a larger number of Congresses, and my focus on moderate polarization, might help bring some additional clarity to the debate over this issue. On the one hand, I certainly have no consistent or systematic evidence of a relationship between productivity and unified party control of government. This is consistent with the position of Krehbiel (1998) whose Pivotal Politics Theory is decidedly nonpartisan. Yet, there is a particular type of divided government that I can imagine might be particularly damaging for legislative productivity. That is, quasi-divided government or split party control of the two legislative chambers in Congress.

Most specifically, and based on some earlier work (Dodd and Schraufnagel 2013), I suspect that pure divided government might not be as harmful as split partisan control of the legislative chambers. My reasoning is that the public can more easily hold accountable both unified and pure divided governments. When there is stalemate in unified governments, it is quite difficult to blame the minority party. Under pure divided government, congressional leaders can blame the president without much difficulty. The chief executive, in turn, can challenge Congress in a manner that the attentive public can easily digest. A similar clear charge of culpability under quasi-divided government is more elusive. This lack of clear accountability may allow Congress to shirk their responsibility to address the topical legislative agenda placed before it.

Considering both measures of productivity that I have created, I do find a statistically significant decrease in productivity associated with quasi-divided government. Considering the *Digest* indicator, if there is no quasi-divided government, there is about a 24 percent chance that a new law passes. This drops to less than 15 percent under quasi-divided government. Considering the Landmark Law consideration, based on the retrospective judgment of history and encyclopedia authors, there are more than 5.5 new Landmark Laws without quasi-divided government, and this drops to less than four under split party control of the two legislative chambers.

Staying with Landmark Laws, the most productive quasi-divided government was the 65th Congress (1917–1919), occurring toward the end of the Progressive Era. In this Congress, there were nine new Landmark Laws chronicled. When the same political party controls both chambers, the most productive Congress is the 73rd (1933–1935), which passes seventeen new Landmark Laws. Unfortunately, some measures of legislative productivity do not stretch back, or forward, far enough to pick up a sufficient sample size of quasi-divided governments, which arguably would prevent their indicators from being able to test the ideas just expressed.[10] Overall, I suggest that quasi-divided governments may be confounding scholarly efforts to settle the debate over divided versus unified government and legislative productivity. In the final chapter, I will begin to wrap up and summarize this analysis of the precepts of LCT, but not without another test of LCT and providing some prescriptive suggestions about how to moderate legislative conflict in Congress, and perhaps legislatures around the world.

NOTES

1. Importantly, when I experiment with using polarization in the House of Representatives or a two-chamber average value, I obtain the same results as it relates to the statistical significance of the conflict considerations. Recall, from chapter 2, the two-chamber specific values are very highly correlated.

2. Using three different sets of assumptions regarding how one should measure the presidential honeymoon, the bivariate relationship with the Clinton-Lapinski measure of Legislative Accomplishment is always statistically indistinguishable from zero.

3. For all the bivariate tests reported in this book, I use a two-tailed test of statistical significance. Because I am anticipating a positive association between Senate Majority Size and productivity, arguably, a one-tailed test would be appropriate. If allowed a one-tailed test, I obtain a statistical link, using the conventional .95 confidence interval, between Senate Majority Size and the Clinton-Lapinski measure of legislative accomplishment.

4. In robustness checks, I do run the productivity models for only those years when the Stimson (1991) public mood variable is available. The conflict considerations still largely perform as hypothesized, albeit there is a reduction in the strength of the statistical relationships.

5. To quote from the Analysis Factor: "The classic example is data from children nested within schools. The dependent variable could be something like math scores, and the predictors a whole host of things measured about the child and the school. Child-level predictors could be things like GPA, grade, and gender. School-level predictors could be things like total enrollment, private vs. public, mean SES. Because multiple children are measured from the same school, their measurements are not independent. Hierarchical modeling takes that into account" (https://www.theanalysisfactor.com/confusing-statistical-term-4-hierarchical-regression-vs-hierarchical-model/, last accessed September 14, 2023). In my case, the Congress is the school and each *Digest* topic are the children.

6. Concerning the measure of moderate polarization, which folds the polarization data, I calculate moderation values, based on the period covered by the measure of productivity. The assumption is that "moderation" is relative to the period of Congressional history one is considering.

7. Values on both conflict measures are standardized (subtract the mean and divide by the standard deviation) and the value of "2" is added to each Congress score to get rid of negative values before the two conflict measures are multiplied.

8. Moving beyond the bivariate tests, I have established the predicted direction of the relationships between the variables discussed. Consequently, I use a one-tailed test to determine statistical significance in the multivariate tests. I also forego distinguishing more precise P-Values, and opt for a the standard consideration of the 95% confidence interval.

9. The lag variable is not statistically significant in the Moderate Polarization model; however, it is in the interaction model. Results reported in table 6.3 are from model runs that include a lagged dependent variable in the model.

10. These caveats or exceptions obviously do not apply to the Clinton-Lapinski measure of Legislative Accomplishment, which has productivity values for the same fifty-nine Congresses that the Landmark Law measure has.

Chapter 7

Managing Conflict in Legislatures

Former president John Kennedy in his 1961 inaugural address made a case for what should lead to an effective legislative process. Specifically, he argues, "So let us begin anew—remembering on both sides that civility is not a sign of weakness, and sincerity is always subject to proof. Let us never negotiate out of fear. But let us never fear to negotiate. Let both sides explore what problems unite us instead of belaboring those problems which divide us" (National Archives). Conflict in legislatures should never be so extreme that we "fear to negotiate." Kennedy's references to "civility" and "sincerity" in political discourse are revealing. He suggests we can be civil while maintaining our convictions. Moreover, sincerity should be "subject to proof," suggesting that we need to earn the trust of others. These normative appeals made by the thirty-fifth president, arguably, are as appropriate today as they were in his time. Indeed, they may be the conditions for an effective legislative process in a republican form of government in any period and especially relevant for contemporary legislatures in the United States.

President Kennedy seems to understand Legislative Conflict Theory (LCT). It is okay to disagree, and we should never fail to negotiate. Perhaps to achieve moderated solutions? To reach this ideal, I suggest one must begin with a comprehensive understanding of the nature of legislative conflict. I imagine levels of tension in the U.S. Congress to be quite a lot like personal differences that exist in most workplaces all over the world and in both private and public sector settings. Prescriptively, there ought to be healthy debate about the proper way to move forward to complete a task, all the while people should find a way to get along reasonably well with one another. What will not work are deep divisions over policy objectives and antagonists willing to engage in spiteful behaviors and other sorted attempts to sabotage the efforts of their workplace colleagues. It is clear that hyper-two-dimensional legislative conflict scenarios can effectively ground democratic governance to a halt.

In this book, I have suggested that there have been periods of U.S. congressional history defined by both too little and too much conflict. The American Political Science Association (1950), writing about the Congresses of the 1940s, suggested that the political parties needed to be more responsible. Their recommendation was greater inter-party difference and discipline. In effect, the call was for greater party system polarization. As we moved into the waning years of the twentieth century, scholars began to argue that the political parties were too polarized (Coleman 1997; Binder 1999) and that super majoritarian institutions and strict party discipline were stifling legislative productivity. I suggest that both groups are correct. Midcentury there was too little legislative conflict and as we closed out the century there was too much.

The puzzle: What changed the level of legislative conflict? Moreover, if there was not enough and then too much, we must have passed through a period of moderate conflict. The analysis reported in this book suggests we did. The 1960s and 1970s were productive. Both Presidents Lyndon Johnson and Richard Nixon are associated with great legislative achievements. Healthcare for the poorest and oldest Americans and clean air and clean water for everyone are just a few of the landmark legislative achievements passed under conditions of moderate legislative conflict in those two decades. The question then becomes, what prompted the increase in conflict sufficient to move us out of the standoffs of the 1940s and 1950s? By extension, what might we do to lower two-dimensional legislative conflict in the third decade of the twenty-first century?

MOVING FROM TOO LITTLE TO MODERATE CONFLICT

I will begin with, perhaps the easier of the two questions. Consulting congressional history, one can gain a better understanding of what happened to break the stranglehold of too little conflict in the mid-twentieth century. I suggest the key was a little intraparty relational conflict, which helped to better define inter-party policy differences. Most specifically, the Democrats, overtime, became more homogeneous in their policy preferences. Some may remember the Democratic Study Group, which formally existed in Congress from 1959 to the early 1990s.[1] The group formed as a liberal counterpoint to conservative leaders of the Democratic Party, and Southern Democrats in particular. Their activities were largely informal in the 1950s, but the group becomes more officially involved throughout the 1960s and into the 1970s.

The Democratic Study Group played a crucial role in provoking intraparty dissension, which ultimately allowed Congress to pass a progressive legislative agenda in the Kennedy, Johnson, and first Nixon Administrations in spite of the opposition of the bipartisan Conservative Coalition. Recall, this coalition brought together the conservative wings of the Republican and Democratic parties to oppose New Deal initiatives and, principally, to stifle progressive reforms addressing the plight of the country's poorer citizens. Seniority norms caused long-serving Southern Democrats to dominate committee leadership positions, enhancing the Conservative Coalition's grip on power. The resolution of Democratic Party internal discord came through the adoption of various reforms to both rules and procedures that slowly but surely chipped away at the capacity of the Southern wing of the Party to block legislation they did not favor. The intra-Democratic Party fissure, which included leadership jousting, was instrumental to an increase in conflict in Congress in the 1960s. Undoubtedly, this also led to the rise of a Southern conservative Republican Party, which in turn, set the stage for the rise of high inter-party conflict in the more contemporary era.

To cite an example of what I am suggesting, consider reporting in the *New York Times* on January 4, 1961, the day after 87th Congress (1961–1963) began. The *Times* reports on an intraparty relational conflict, which took place in the House of Representatives the previous day.[2] Speaker Sam Rayburn (D-TX) and Minority Leader Charles Halleck (R-IN) proclaimed, publicly, their desire to work for "responsible party government" a not-so-veiled reference to the need for better party discipline or more party polarization. The *Times* reports that, at the same time, "Behind the scenes . . . a liberal-conservative fight for control of the [House] Rules Committee continued unabated."[3] Speaker Rayburn, in order to appease liberal Democrats, removed William Colmer (D-MS), a conservative Southern, from a seat on the all-important committee. The intention, according to the *Times*, was to "create a Rules Committee majority favoring critical parts of President-elect John F. Kennedy's program."[4] In the same article, the *Times* reports about intra-Democratic Party squabbling in the Senate over leadership positions and reform of Senate Rule XXII, which Southern Democrats routinely used to block progress on comprehensive civil rights legislation.

In chapter 1, I elaborated briefly on centralizing constitutional provisions that can prompt efficiency, such as the designation of chamber leaders and majority rule stipulations. On the other side of the same coin, bicameralism and federalism, established by the Constitution, decentralize decision-making and increase the representative quality of the national government. Similarly, House and Senate rules can create a back and forth, as it relates to the centralization of authority, which can change the nature of legislative conflict. Rule changes rarely cause Congress to pivot on a dime, but given some time, the changes can lend themselves to more or less efficiency, or representativeness, in a manner sufficient to change the level of internal discord. In trying to understand the move from too little to moderate conflict in the 1960s, it is quite easy to recognize intraparty splits causing caustic intraparty relationships, which led to rule changes, which, in turn, prompted legislative innovation.

Unfortunately, the rule changes may have gone too far. The Legislative Reorganization Act of 1970 (P.L. 91–510) decentralized representation even further. The Act, which focused mainly on the procedures that govern committee activities, decreased the power of committee chairs, created more subcommittees, empowered committee members from the minority party, and created a more individualistic Congress (Patterson, Loewenberg, and Jewell 1983; Quirk 1991). The Republican Party would need to weather the Watergate scandal before it could take full advantage of the opportunity to become a co-equal political party, but once the party's Southern strategy was in full force in the 1980s, the party began to share legislative supremacy. Majority control of the two chambers of Congress began to oscillate, beginning in the 1990s. Importantly, the hyper-conflict of the twenty-first century was born. The task now becomes how to rein things back in. Rules changes might help, but just as likely, it will require quality leadership and/or the moderating influences of minor party members in Congress, who might serve as policy brokers.

MOVING FROM TOO MUCH TO MODERATE CONFLICT

How can the severe legislative conflict of twenty-first century Congresses be reduced? There are at least two congressional eras that witnessed hyper-legislative conflict to consult. The first is the pre–Civil War antebellum Congresses of the 1830s through the 1850s. Unfortunately, one must recognize, in this case, that the legislative conflict of the era ultimately ends in civil war. Yet, tensions over slavery existed at the country's founding and the Alien and Sedition Acts of the John Adams Administration fueled instances of factional conflict in the early years of the republic. Yet, the first half of the nineteenth century witnesses' important legislative achievements. I suggest temporary reductions in legislative conflict, orchestrated by effective congressional leaders, prompt these statutory successes. Put differently, attenuation of conflict occurs because effective congressional leaders find ways to broker compromises. The second instance of hyper-conflict is the Congresses of the late nineteenth century. In this case, a minor political party, and a partisan realignment, played important roles in mediating conflict and prompting policy innovations. Notwithstanding, the value of more women in Congress and more members with state legislative experience, as we learned in chapter 4, the role of leaders in the antebellum period and a minor party in the late nineteenth century Congresses, suggest other possible solutions to the severe conflict occurring in contemporary Congresses.

The Antebellum Period

Many of the pre-Civil War Congresses, after the election of Andrew Jackson in 1828, experienced hyper-legislative conflict. The party average DW-NOMINATE scores and the caning of Charles Sumner (R-MA) by Preston Brooks (D-SC), in 1856, confirm that two-dimensional conflict was high (Hull 2010). In this era, the thrice elected speaker of the House of Representatives Henry Clay (Whig-KY) was instrumental in forging compromises between factions in Congress, leading to policy successes. Notably, some members of the largely regional factions would just as soon duel with one another as shake hands. In addition, John Quincy Adams, a former president, becomes a member of the House of Representatives, during this time period, and his stewardship was likewise influential in reducing conflict in Congress in a manner that prompted legislative productivity. Adams famously noted, "To believe all men honest would be folly. To believe none so is something worse."[5] His position on honesty is perfectly consistent with the precepts of LCT that suggest members of Congress should negotiate legislation, but do so charily.

Many refer to Henry Clay as the Great Compromiser. As a political leader, his skills of negotiation and compromise proved invaluable in helping to hold the country together for the first half of the nineteenth century. His compromises quelled regionalism and balanced states' rights and national interests. He is associated with considerable landmark legislative achievements while serving as speaker of the House of Representatives. For instance, considering the Missouri Compromise, Clay skillfully engineered separate votes on controversial measures that admitted Maine as a free state, Missouri as a slave state, and made all Western territories north of Missouri's southern border "free soil." In addition, Clay was largely responsible for getting the General Survey Act of 1924 passed, which represents the first significant infrastructure bill intended to promote commerce among the American states. However, it was his role in the Senate in the 1830s and 1840s that is, perhaps, most remarkable for diffusing legislative conflict.

The United States Senate website argues that the Kentuckian was "a pivotal Senate leader during the antebellum era, a period in Senate history marked by heated debates over slavery and territorial expansion." Senate archives continue, "Clay helped guide a fragile Union through several critical impasses. As senator, he forged the Compromise of 1850 to maintain the Union."[6] Notably, upon his death in 1852, Clay thought the Union had survived without war. As evidence of his greatness as a negotiator and conflict mediator, President Abraham Lincoln once told a sculptor carving his likeness that he "almost worshiped Henry Clay" and called Clay "my beau of a statesman, for whom I fought all my humble life" (Portteus 2020). The career of Henry Clay points to the possibility that severe conflict in the 2020s might attenuate through effective leadership. More evidence of this possibility comes from another prominent political leader in the Antebellum Era, a former president and son of one of the country's founders.

John Quincy Adams served as president of the United States from 1825 to 1829. Then, in 1830, the constituents of the district, which included Plymouth, Massachusetts, elected him to the House of Representatives, where he served for the remainder of his life. Historians routinely refer to him as a "powerful leader."[7] Above all, he fought against limits on civil liberties, especially as it related to the enslaved population. In 1836, Southern members of Congress passed a "gag rule" providing that the House automatically table any petition intended to restrict slavery. Adams tirelessly fought the rule for eight years until finally he obtained its repeal. His stature as a former president certainly added gravitas to his remarks in the Lower Chamber, and like Clay, Adams helped to attenuate sectional conflict at a time when incidents of relational conflict were nearly an everyday occurrence in both chambers of Congress. In 1848, Adams collapsed on the floor of the House from a stroke; fellow members carried him to the Speaker's Room, where two days later he died. To the end, "Old Man Eloquent" fought for what he considered right.[8]

The service of both Clay and Adams speaks to the role of competent congressional leadership. Notably, both men died about a decade before conflict in Congress broke loose in a manner, which triggers the U.S. Civil War. While they served, their stewardship managed to hold the nation together, consistently moderating legislative conflict and finding ways to negotiate cooperation. One might argue that Adams was more principled and less likely to seek compromise than Clay. Yet, it seems Clay was righteous in one important manner: his first objective was a "more perfect union." In 1957, a Senate committee headed by John F. Kennedy and charged with the task of honoring its most distinguished past members named Clay the greatest senator in the history of the United States.[9] He earns this recognition, to be certain, for his ability to reduce legislative conflict in an era of severe partisan and sectional discord. Next, it is possible to scrutinize another period of hyperconflict in Congress: the Gilded Age, to appreciate what other conditions can possibly reduce legislative conflict to more manageable levels.

Hyper-Legislative Conflict in the 1880s and 1890s

Near the end of the Gilded Age (1877–1900) in the United States, the Populist Party began to gain representation in Congress. From figure 2.3, in chapter 2, we can see this was a period of high party polarization between Democrats and Republicans. Perhaps too high. During the 144 years studied in this book, only the twenty-first century Congresses are more polarized than those at the turn of the twentieth century are. Corresponding to the polarization of the era was the emergence of the Populist Party, which after the 1896 elections held 22 of the 357 seats in the House of Representatives and five of the 90 Senate seats. The Populist Party, originally called the People's National Party (Hild 2007), called for a graduated national income tax, the direct election of U.S. senators, adoption of the Australian ("secret") ballot, a term limit for the U.S. president, and an eight-hour workday for government employees (Goodwyn 1978). Perhaps not coincidentally, all the legislative initiatives just mentioned, which were part of the Populist Party platform in 1896, most people today would consider good public policy.

The Populist Party was able to maintain membership in six consecutive Congresses in an era of intense two-party polarization. Many Populist candidates benefited from fusion practices, which allowed their candidates to run as both a Populist and as either a Democrat or a Republican Party candidate (Hunt 2003). In the South, Populists fused with Republican Party candidates and in other regions of the country with Democratic Party candidates. While overall, the Populists were more closely aligned with the Democratic Party, based on DW-NOMINATE scores, they were more moderate in their voting behavior than the average Democrat. This fits the argument that Populist Party members were in a position to broker compromises. Indeed, while Populists served in Congress, they often attenuated legislative conflict, bringing it down to the moderate level we have learned can be effective.

There is good evidence that some Republicans ran as Populist fusion candidates in the South, to help break up Democratic Party dominance in the region, but also to cause a break in inter-party regional hostilities.[10] Albert Taylor Goodwyn, a Populist Party member from Alabama, had an ideology score in the 54th Congress (1895–1897) very close to the Republican Party mean. Differentiating himself from Democrats and his fellow Populists, Goodwyn was a former captain in the Confederate Army, but later in life worked steadfastly to unite both sides of the country and create a more peaceful post-Civil War era. He was the first representative of a Confederate veterans organization invited to a presidential inauguration.[11] This particular Populist Party member was certainly interested in reducing conflict.

Ultimately, we see a party realignment in 1896 (Kawato 1987) a time when Republican Party dominance supplants intense two-party competition. Others argue that the change was not abrupt and took place over several election cycles, bleeding into the early twentieth century and the Progressive Era, defined by significant legislative achievement (Stonecash and Silina 2005). Another minor party, the Progressive Party, was an important influence in this era, as well. The success of minor parties, actually gaining seats in Congress, and the partisan realignment may not be mutually exclusive events. The role of minor parties, capable of splitting the difference between Democratic and Republican Party stalwarts, is a possible prescription for breaking hyper-two-party polarization in contemporary Congresses. Fundamental changes in election law are likely necessary to allow minor party success in the modern era (Schraufnagel 2011, Chapter 6) and this is a tall order. In any event, it is useful to recognize the possibility, which might initiate the grueling process of election reform.

In all, the solutions to severe legislative conflict, given the two historical examples just highlighted, are distinct. In the first case, the reduction in conflict occurs ad hoc as the result of the work of competent congressional leaders, in particular, Henry Clay and John Quincy Adams. In the second incident, minor party involvement was instrumental. In particular, the moderating influence of Populist Party members at the turn of the twentieth century helped to usher in a new era of more moderate two-party conflict. A level of conflict, which was able to prompt Progressive Era reforms such as child labor laws, safer working conditions, and women's suffrage.

In all of this, I think it is important to consider the role played by individual members of Congress. Whether it be Henry Clay, John Quincy Adams, or Albert Goodwyn, the Populist from Alabama. The role of individual members in helping to shape legislative conflict can be significant. Importantly, it is not always the case that one would wish for members, or leaders, to reduce conflict. The need to reduce or increase legislative conflict is era dependent. Recall, when conflict was lower in the 1930s, an antagonist like Huey Long (D-LA) was a force prompting grand legislative achievements.

As a last test of LCT, I move to offer four brief case studies of individual members of Congress. Each was a notorious norm-breaker. Two of them served when Congress was highly polarized and two in eras where polarization was either waning or at a low level. LCT suggests the agitators will be less effective when polarization is high and more effective when it is declining, or at a low point. If these case studies are revealing, the research will establish the important role played by the individuals who populate congressional chambers. We will then have a better understanding of how to fix the "broken branch" (Mann and Ornstein 2006). Namely, recruiting the right type of people to serve in Congress.

THE LEGISLATIVE EFFECTIVENESS OF THE NORM-BREAKERS: DIFFERENT POLARIZATION SCENARIOS

As noted, I chose four members who served at times of both high and low party system polarization to test the contention that the value of norm-breaking uncivil behavior will vary depending on the polarization context. I chose the four members from the top twenty-five norm-breakers who have served during the 144-year period studied. Newspaper reports have implicated all four members in incivilities at least eight different times. As noted in chapter 2, party polarization overtime takes on a distinctive U-shaped, with the late years of the nineteenth and twentieth centuries experiencing higher polarization and the middle years, sometimes referred to as the textbook era, witnessing more across party cooperation (Pearson and Schickler 2009, 1239), or possible partisan elite collusion. I chose one highly uncivil member from the late nineteenth century (Roscoe Conkling R-NY), one from the early twentieth century when polarization was waning (Benjamin Tillman D-SC), one from the mid-twentieth century (Carter Glass D-VA) categorized by low polarization, and one from the contemporary period (Ted Cruz R-TX) characterized by high party system polarization.

LCT suggests norm-breakers serving when party polarization has been declining, or established at a low level, will be more productive. On the other hand, if conflict is already high, the norm breakers will be detrimental to the effective operation of the legislative branch. Conkling and Cruz both serve in Congress when polarization is high, and I expect them to be toxic and less effective. Tillman served when polarization was waning and Glass when polarization was near its nadir, and I anticipate these senators will associate with landmark legislative productivity.

Roscoe Conkling

Conkling was a prominent figure in New York politics, serving as both a representative and a senator in the second half of the nineteenth century. It is important to consider that Conkling was serving at the time of the Senate impeachment trial of President Andrew Johnson and during hotly contested partisan debates over Reconstruction policies, in the aftermath of the Civil War. With this backdrop, his acerbic demeanor ramped up conflict when there was already plenty of partisan disagreement. Conkling frequently clashed with his fellow Republicans and, specifically, Senator Reuben Fenton (R-NY), which led to an enduring personal rivalry.

In the newspapers consulted, I find thirteen articles that mention Conkling engaging in norm-breaking incivilities. As Maslin-Wicks (2007) observes,

Conkling's deficiency in social aptitude, coupled with his propensity for hostility and vindictiveness, presented challenges for him in building trusting relationships with colleagues and constituents. In the highly polarized post-Civil War era, his demeanor clearly hampers his ability to foster alliances and cultivate influence within the Republican Party, or more broadly, in Congress.

One instance illustrating Conkling's disregard for Senate norms was his interaction with Senator Lucius Quintus Lamar (D-GA), which involved "violent and offensive language beyond anything ever before heard in that body."[12] A *Washington Post* article notes that "there have been many days in the Senate when Conkling[s] manner toward other senators [ranged from] constant provocation to assault."[13] Notably, his norm-breaking incivilities included attacks on both fellow Republicans and members of the Democratic opposition. There is considerable evidence that his incivilities stem largely from personal conflicts rather than policy disagreements. The type of conflict Conkling was fueling is not the type that effectively structures meaningful policy debate. In the later stages of his career, he played primarily a negative legislative role, opposing paper currency, berating civil service reform, and defending other status quo policies (Maslin-Wicks 2007). In sum, in an era characterized by high levels of party polarization, Conkling's ability to promote meaningful policy change is absent.

Benjamin Tillman

The second case is Senator Benjamin Ryan Tillman, a significant figure in South Carolina politics and the United States Senate. Born near Trenton, Edgefield County, South Carolina, Tillman served as the Governor of South Carolina from 1890 to 1894, overseeing the establishment of Clemson College and Winthrop College. His constituents elected him as a Democrat to the U.S. Senate in 1894, and he held the seat until his death in 1918. His tenure was tumultuous and, ultimately, the Senate censured him in 1902 for assaulting another member on the chamber floor.[14]

Senator Tillman was a known norm-breaker and controversial figure in the Senate. Labeled a demagogue, he earn the nickname "Pitchfork Ben" for his cruel and obscene attacks on political opponents. Recall the story from chapter 1, when Tillman became embroiled in a dispute with his colleague Senator John L. McLaurin (D-SC), whom he accused of lacking party discipline. Newspapers reported that the fisticuffs were the worst show of violence since the caning of Senator Charles Sumner by Representative Preston Brooks (D-SC), in 1856.[15] Yet, the public perceived Tillman as a fierce advocate for the common person, and he was particularly popular in rural America.

During the period that Tillman was serving, party polarization was declining from late nineteenth century highs (see figure 2.3). In fact, during the 1912 presidential election, commentators found it difficult to find appreciable differences between the issue positions of former Republican President Theodore Roosevelt and Democratic Party candidate Woodrow Wilson.[16] As an example of Tillman's effectiveness as a lawmaker during this time-period, one only need to consider the Tillman Act of 1907, which was the first-ever national campaign-finance-reform legislation. The legislation prohibited corporations and national banks from contributing money to federal election campaigns.

A year earlier, Tillman was instrumental in passing the Hepburn Rate Act, intended to regulate railroad pricing. Republican President Theodore Roosevelt supported the measure, but his Republican brethren in the Senate did not. Senator Nelson Aldrich (R-RI), an opponent of the legislation and party leader in the Senate, assigned the management of the bill to Tillman. Aldrich hoped that Tillman's involvement would lead to the bill's defeat. However, to Aldrich's surprise, Tillman approached the task with sobriety and competence, and successfully navigated the bill through the legislative process. The Hepburn Bill garnered significant public attention, and Tillman earned considerable respect for his role in the legislation's passage. Still more, in his last years in the Senate, Tillman facilitated allocating millions of military dollars to South Carolina to promote the economic well-being of his constituents and the state of South Carolina (Kantrowitz 2016).

Fading and low party polarization levels during the early years of the twentieth century arguably contributed to Senator Tillman's effectiveness as a lawmaker. With lower ideological divisions, Tillman's rabble-rousing style helped to bring salience to important issues and effectively raised public awareness of the need for action while structuring debate in a manner that helped to define alternative policy options. Once the table was set, the lower levels of across-party animosity allowed for productive collaboration and consensus-building. Tillman, somewhat unexpectedly, was able to garner sufficient support for many prized legislative initiatives. Arguably, depolarization and a shift in the political landscape required a norm-breaker to highlight policy options and, ultimately, to increase landmark legislative productivity.

Carter Glass

A representative and a senator, Carter Glass was a prominent Virginia Democrat and a distinguished figure in mid-twentieth century American politics. After serving in the Lower Chamber, in 1918, President Woodrow Wilson appointed Glass Secretary of the Treasury, a position he held until 1920 when he resigned to assume one of Virginia's two U.S. Senate seats, where he served until his passing in 1946.[17] His Senate years represent the low point of party system polarization during the period studied in this book (see figure 2.3).

Known for his frequent use of vitriolic rhetoric aimed at political opponents, I found eight mentions of Senator Glass engaging in norm-breaking incivilities in the newspaper articles consulted. He was a segregationist, a strong supporter of Jim Crowe laws intended to disenfranchise Black voters, and much of his relational conflict had racist overtones. Yet, reviewing the incidents, one notices that, in most cases, he is not the initiator of the personal attacks. Yet, he certainly had a caustic and vindictive way of responding to any criticism. During one of the incidents, a visibly angry Glass railed at his fellow Democrats, calling the bill they supported an "uneconomic, unpatriotic species of privilege." He continued noting that Democratic supporters of the legislation were "deserters of democratic doctrines."[18] Notably, fellow Democrats were often the victims of his verbal haranguing, which obviously distinguishes the type of conflict he was responsible for from party system polarization, defined by inter-party policy differences, or affective polarization defined by disgust for the opposing political party.

Despite the media coverage his antics brought, contemporaries often praised his caustic language as an appealing trait (Shaw 2020). Many viewed him as an adept legislator who played a key role in passing significant legislation during his time in Congress. Despite his reservations about certain aspects of financial regulation, one of his most significant accomplishments was the passage of the Glass-Steagall Act of 1933, which established the Federal Deposit Insurance Corporation and separated the activities of commercial and investment banks. Earlier, Glass helped guide through Congress President Wilson's proposal for the Federal Reserve System, which Congress established in 1913. For his long support of the Federal Reserve, many refer to Glass as the "Father of the Federal Reserve."[19]

In the absence of heightened polarization, Senator Glass' propensity for intraparty relational conflict, his strong convictions, and persuasive rhetoric allowed him to build consensus and drive important legislative initiatives home. The low polarized atmosphere fostered an environment conducive to productive collaboration and compromise once an agitator such as Glass had effectively established policy options and opportunities. Senator Glass's policy prescriptions often transcended traditional party lines, and he was able to garner bipartisan support for his policy proposals. His obvious racist attitudes aside, in the uniquely depolarized context in which he served, Senator Glass demonstrated effectiveness as a legislator, leaving a legacy of impactful legislation that shaped the nation's financial system.

Ted Cruz

Rafael Edward "Ted" Cruz is a Senator representing the state of Texas. Cruz graduated from Princeton University in 1992 with a Bachelor of Arts degree and later earned his *Juris Doctorate* degree from Harvard University in 1995. He gained valuable experience as a law clerk to Chief Justice William Rehnquist and served in various roles, including associate deputy attorney general at the U.S. Department of Justice and director of the Office of Policy Planning at the Federal Trade Commission. From 2003 to 2008, Cruz held the position of solicitor general of Texas.[20] In all, Cruz has sufficient pedigree, both in terms of academic and professional experience, to be an effective legislator.

Notably, Cruz is widely recognized as a norm breaker, serving in a highly polarized era. There are nine mentions of the junior senator from Texas flouting Senate norms from the 113th (2013–2015) his first Congress, through the 116th (2019–2021) Congress. Perhaps best exemplifying Cruz's harshness is his notorious norm-breaking act when he repeatedly called his Senate Leader, Mitch McConnell (R-KY), a liar on the floor of the chamber.[21] The topic was the floor amendment process and Cruz declared, "Like Saint Peter [McConnell] repeated [the lie] three times." According to Samuel Popkin (2021), Cruz considers the Republican Party a party of one, relying on a strategy of Republican legislative failure, to make the case for his reckless style and approach to lawmaking. Importantly, for my purpose, during his decade-long tenure in the Senate, Senator Cruz has sponsored very few original bills, and those he has sponsored, according to legislative effectiveness scoring protocols, have not been "significant" (Volden and Wiseman 2018). Instead of focusing on passing legislation, Cruz seems to employ a unique strategy of "winning by losing," which involves hogging the spotlight as the most extreme person in the room (Popkin 2021, 76).

When comparing Senator Cruz to Senate colleagues, it is enlightening to consider the other Senator from Texas, in the contemporary period. John Cornyn, also a Republican from the Lone Star state. Cornyn has taken a decidedly civil approach to lawmaking. For instance, Cornyn does not appear in any of the newspaper searches used to find incidents of relational conflict. In a highly polarized era, Cornyn's tact has resulted in considerable legislative accomplishment. During his tenure in the Senate, he has successfully worked to pass seven bipartisan bills,[22] while Cruz from the same political party and the same state has passed none. Serving during a time of high polarization the incivilities, and penchant for norm breaking, that have marked Senator Cruz's legislative career has hindered his ability to advance any significant or landmark legislation.

These sketches of four notable members of Congress, spanning different periods of congressional history, defined by varying levels of party polarization, provide insight into the value of LCT in explaining legislative productivity. Senator Conkling (R-NY) is a poster child for relational conflict and served in an era characterized by high party conflict, ultimately rendering him ineffective in marshalling significant legislative outcomes. In contrast, Senator Tillman (D-SC), despite his association with the dark legacy of racism and white supremacy, managed to leave a significant mark by championing campaign finance reform. His success, was arguably, aided by the waning of party polarization, which occurs during his time in office. Similarly, Senator Glass (D-VA), also racist and caustic, made significant contributions in the finance policy arena. Senator Glass's intraparty incivilities seemed to help him navigate the political landscape and advance crucial legislation at a time marked by a base level of polarized politics. Lastly, Senator Ted Cruz (R-TX) has emerged as a highly uncivil figure and his confrontational style, clearly, has hindered his ability to foster collaboration and compromise in contemporary, highly polarized, Congresses. These contrasting profiles demonstrate how the interplay of incivilities and polarization can effect legislative success and shape the complex legacies and reputations of norm-breakers in Congress.

SUMMARY

Missing in much contemporary discussion of the legislative process in the United States is a full appreciation of the effect that norm-breaking relational conflict has on the legislative process. This book has attempted to fill that gap. Undoubtedly, the great difficulty of measuring a dense social science concept like "relational conflict" is a core reason for the minimal amount of scholarly attention this has received. Yet, my ideas about legislative conflict are becoming more fashionable. Rasmus Skytte, and others, attempt to "disentangle the effects of the two dimensions of conflict" (2020, 4). Unfortunately, much of this work builds on what scholars refer to as "affective polarization" or the degree to which politicians and citizens have negative feelings toward the opposing party (Rogowski and Sutherland 2016; Mason 2016; Luttig 2017). These negative views could certainly lead to relational conflict of the type discussed throughout this book. However, just like distinct roll call voting, affective polarization is not the same as relational conflict in Congress. Affective polarization, or downbeat feelings about the opposing party, is neither a necessary nor a sufficient condition to cause someone to scream "You Lie" at their own party's Senate leader or for two rank-and-file members from the same political party to squabble and call each other names like "little bitch," as occurred in the 118th Congress (2021–2023). My scouring of newspaper coverage of relational conflict suggests that only a little more than 50 percent of the norm-breaking incivilities involve individuals from opposing political parties. Most notably, affective polarization is about a feeling and relational conflict is an overt act.

I suggest it is time for political scientists, studying Congress, to recognize what organizational scholars have been discussing for years. People who fundamentally disagree on how to complete a task can get along with one another in the workplace. In this case, I am referring to the congressional workplace. Moreover, people who fundamentally agree about many different policy prescriptions can get cantankerous, spiteful, and belligerent toward one another. Yes, members of Congress from the same political party sometimes find it very difficult to get along. Perhaps this is especially the case, when their co-partisans are threatening their delusions of self-importance. I have long imagined that we need a new breed of legislator in our time, a group humbler and more prone to embrace compromise and cooperation. The hyper-conflict of twenty-first century Congresses begs mitigation. More effective leaders, a modicum of minor party representation, more former state legislators, and perhaps more women serving in Congress point to possible solutions. Yet, nothing is likely to change until congressional scholars, the attentive public, and voters begin to appreciate the precepts of LCT and recognize the nature of two-dimensional legislative conflict. This book hopes to serve as a wakeup call for moderation.

NOTES

1. After the 1970s, the Democratic Study Group focused on legislative service, disseminating detailed written materials to members of the House about upcoming legislation and pending policy proposals.

2. Russell Baker. "Congress Opens with Conflicts on Procedures." *New York Times*. January 4, 1961, 1.

3. Russell Baker. "Congress Opens with Conflicts on Procedures." *New York Times*. January 4, 1961, 1.

4. Russell Baker. "Congress Opens with Conflicts on Procedures." *New York Times*. January 4, 1961, 1.

5. *Forbes* Quotes, https://www.forbes.com/quotes/5421/ (last accessed September 14, 2023).

6. United States Senate, https://www.senate.gov/senators/FeaturedBios/Featured_Bio_Clay.htm#:~:text=He%20was%20elected%20to%20the,quickly%20rose%20to%20become%20Speaker (last accessed September 15, 2023).

7. The White House, https://www.whitehouse.gov/about-the-white-house/presidents/john-quincy-adams/#:~:text=In%201848%2C%20he%20collapsed%20on,for%20what%20he%20considered%20right (last accessed September 15, 2023).

8. Massachusetts Historical Society, https://www.masshist.org/publications/jqa-diaries/index.php/headnotes/old-man-eloquent (last accessed September 15, 2023).

9. American History from Revolution to Reconstruction and beyond, https://www.let.rug.nl/usa/biographies/henry-clay/ (last accessed September 15, 2023).

10. Editorial, *New York Times*. December 25, 1894, 9.
11. Editorial, *New York Times*, July 2, 1931, 27.
12. Editorial, *New York Times*, June 10, 1879, 1.
13. Editorial, *Washington Post*, June 10, 1879, 2.
14. Tillman, Benjamin Ryan (1847–1918). *Biographical Directory of the United States Congress 1774—Present*, https://bioguideretro.congress.gov/Home/MemberDetails?memIndex=T000274 (last accessed May 24, 2023).
15. Editorial, *Washington Post*, February 23, 1902, 1; Editorial, *New York Times*, February 23, 1902, 1.
16. *Bill of Rights in Action: Constitutional Rights Foundation*, https://www.crf-usa.org/images/pdf/gates/election_1912.pdf (last accessed May 31, 2023).
17. Glass, Carter (1858–1946). *Biographical Directory of the United States Congress 1774—Present*, https://bioguideretro.congress.gov/Home/MemberDetails?memIndex=G000232 (last accessed May 24, 2023).
18. Editorial, Washington Post, June 23, 1926, 9.
19. *Department of the Treasury*, https://home.treasury.gov/about/history/prior-secretaries/carter-glass-1918-1920 (last accessed May 31, 2023).
20. Cruz, Rafael Edward (Ted). *Biographical Directory of the United States Congress 1774—Present*, https://bioguideretro.congress.gov/Home/MemberDetails?memIndex=C001098 (last accessed May 24, 2023).
21. DeBonis, Mike, *Washington Post*, July 24, 2015, A4.
22. These include notable legislation such as the CyberTipline Modernization Act of 2018 and the Corrections Act in the 115th Congress (2017–2019), along with the Federal Officers and Employees Protection Act in the 117th Congress (2021–2023).

Appendix A

Table A.1 Members Mentioned in Multiple Newspaper Articles (Referring to Chapter 4)

Last Name	First Name	State	Year 1st Implicated	Senator *	Count
Tillman	Benjamin	SC	1916	1	32
McCarthy	Joseph	WI	1955	1	30
Hoar	George	MA	1902	1	18
Long	Huey	LA	1933	1	18
Conkling	Roscoe	NY	1881	1	14
Heflin	James	AL	1929	1	12
Helms	Jesse	NC	1999	1	12
Reed	James	MO	1929	1	12
Morgan	John	AL	1902	1	10
Cannon	Joseph	IL	1909	0	9
Reed	Thomas	ME	1898	0	9
Reid	Harry	NV	2013	1	9
Bailey	Joseph	TX	1909	1	8
Glass	Carter	VA	1939	1	8
Hill	Benjamin	GA	1881	1	8
Ingalls	John	KS	1888	1	8
Morse	Wayne	OR	1957	1	8
Blanton	Thomas	TX	1936	0	7
Cruz	Ted	TX	2013	1	7
Gingrich	Newt	GA	1996	0	7
Lamar	Lucius	MS	1883	1	7
McKellar	Kenneth	TN	1947	1	7
Riddleberger	Harrison	VA	1888	1	7
Armey	Richard	TX	1995	0	6
Blaine	James	ME	1879	1	6
Butler	Matthew	SC	1894	1	6
Dornan	Robert	CA	1996	0	6
Edmunds	George	VT	1886	1	6

(continued)

Table A.1 Members Mentioned in Multiple Newspaper Articles (Referring to Chapter 4) (Continued)

Last Name	First Name	State	Year 1st Implicated	Senator *	Count
Hill	David	NY	1896	1	6
Minton	Sherman	IN	1940	1	6
Pelosi	Nancy	CA	2014	0	6
Spooner	John	WI	1907	1	6
Williams	John Sharp	MS	1919	1	6
Allen	William	NE	1900	1	5
Beck	James	KY	1889	1	5
Kennedy	Robert	OH	1890	0	5
Kennedy	Edward	MA	2004	1	5
McConnell	Addison (Mitch)	KY	2013	1	5
McLaurin	John	SC	1902	1	5
Robinson	Joseph	AR	1937	1	5
Sargent	Aaron	CA	1879	1	5
Schumer	Charles	NY	2018	1	5
Thomas	William	CA	2003	0	5
Wilson	Addison (Joe)	SC	2009	0	5
Zioncheck	Marion	WA	1936	0	5
Byrd	Robert	WV	2008	1	4
Cameron	James Donald	PA	1881	1	4
Grosvenor	Charles	OH	1900	0	4
Harris	Isham	TN	1894	1	4
Hewitt	Abram	NY	1882	0	4
Long	Russell	LA	1967	1	4
Norris	George	NE	1938	1	4
Pepper	Claude	FL	1939	1	4
Sparks	William	IL	1880	0	4
Teller	Henry	CO	1902	1	4
Voorhees	Daniel	IN	1888	1	4
Watson	Thomas	GA	1922	1	4
Wolcott	Edward	CO	1900	1	4
Ashurst	Henry	AZ	1928	1	3
Bilbo	Theodore	MS	1937	1	3
Blackburn	Joseph	KY	1887	1	3
Blair	Henry	NH	1888	1	3
Call	Wilkinson	FL	1894	1	3
Chandler	William	NH	1894	1	3
Conger	Omar	MI	1880	0	3
Cotton	Tom	AR	2020	1	3
Crisp	Charles	GA	1895	0	3
Dawes	Henry	MA	1882	1	3
DeLay	Tom	TX	2006	0	3
Dirksen	Everett	IL	1963	1	3
Dole	Robert	KS	1988	1	3
Frist	William	TN	2005	1	3

(continued)

Appendix A 125

Table A.1 Members Mentioned in Multiple Newspaper Articles (Referring to Chapter 4) (Continued)

Last Name	First Name	State	Year 1st Implicated	Senator *	Count
Gaetz	Matthew	FL	2019	0	3
Garfield	James	OH	1879	0	3
Gorman	Arthur	MD	1906	1	3
Gray	George	DE	1894	1	3
Hepburn	William	IA	1909	0	3
Hiscock	Frank	NY	1890	1	3
Hoffman	Clare	MI	1948	0	3
Holt	Rush	WV	1940	1	3
Johnson	Henry	IN	1899	0	3
Jordan	Jim	OH	2019	0	3
Lentz	John	OH	1900	0	3
Lodge	Henry	MA	1924	1	3
Logan	John	IL	1886	1	3
Lott	Chester (Trent)	MS	2002	1	3
Macon	Robert	AR	1910	0	3
McCumber	Porter	ND	1921	1	3
Mitchell	John	OR	1888	1	3
Money	Hernando	MS	1898	0	3
O'Connor	John	NY	1936	0	3
Pettigrew	Richard	SD	1900	1	3
Plumb	Preston	KS	1890	1	3
Rankin	John	MS	1946	0	3
Robeson	George	NJ	1882	0	3
Schiff	Adam	CA	2017	0	3
Smith	Ellison	SC	1940	1	3
Taft	Robert	OH	1953	1	3
Thurmond	Strom	SC	1980	1	3
Van Wyck	Charles	NE	1887	1	3
Vest	George	MO	1894	1	3
Walker	Robert	PA	1986	0	3
Weaver	James	IA	1880	0	3
Weicker	Lowell	CT	1980	1	3
Wheeler	Burton	MT	1937	1	3
Bailey	Josiah	NC	1939	1	2
Bayard	Thomas	DE	1879	1	2
Berry	James	AR	1903	1	2
Beveridge	Albert	IN	1907	1	2
Boland	Patrick	PA	1936	0	2
Brooks	Jack	TX	1994	0	2
Bruce	William	MD	1929	1	2
Burke	Edward	NE	1937	1	2
Capehart	Homer	IN	1957	1	2
Clark	Joel	MO	1939	1	2
Clayton	Henry	AL	1908	0	2
Clymer	Hiester	PA	1880	0	2

(continued)

Table A.1 Members Mentioned in Multiple Newspaper Articles (Referring to Chapter 4) (Continued)

Last Name	First Name	State	Year 1st Implicated	Senator *	Count
Coburn	Tom	OK	2008	1	2
Cockrell	Francis	MO	1893	1	2
Cox	Samuel	NY	1882	0	2
Cramton	Louis	MI	1931	0	2
Dalzell	John	PA	1906	0	2
Daschle	Thomas	SD	2001	1	2
De Armond	David	MO	1908	0	2
Dies	Martin	TX	1942	0	2
Dieterich	William	IL	1938	1	2
Doggett	Lloyd	TX	1997	0	2
Ekwall	William	OR	1936	0	2
Ernst	Richard	KY	1925	1	2
Fess	Simeon	OH	1934	1	2
Flanders	Ralph	VT	1954	1	2
Frear	James A.	WI	1928	0	2
Frye	William	ME	1902	1	2
Gaines	John	TN	1909	0	2
George	Walter	GA	1930	1	2
Gohmert	Louie	TX	2019	0	2
Gramm	William Phil	TX	1985	1	2
Guffey	Joseph	PA	1943	1	2
Hale	Eugene	ME	1900	1	2
Harrison	"Pat" Byron	MS	1932	1	2
Hastert	Dennis	IL	2004	0	2
Hawley	Joseph	CT	1900	1	2
Issa	Darrell	CA	2014	0	2
Johnson	Hiram	CA	1941	1	2
Keifer	Joseph	OH	1883	0	2
Kerr	Robert	OK	1957	1	2
La Follette	Robert	WI	1922	1	2
Lamar	William	FL	1905	0	2
Lenroot	Irvine	WI	1922	1	2
Littlefield	Charles	ME	1905	0	2
Lucas	Scott	IL	1949	1	2
McCarran	Patrick	NV	1952	1	2
McInnis	Scott	CO	2003	0	2
Michel	Robert	IL	1992	0	2
Miller	Samuel	PA	1882	0	2
Miller	Warner	NY	1887	1	2
Morrison	William	IL	1884	0	2
Moses	George	NH	1933	1	2
Mundt	Karl	SD	1962	1	2
Neely	Matthew	WV	1949	1	2
Norton	Patrick	ND	1917	0	2
Patman	John William	TX	1972	0	2

(continued)

Table A.1 Members Mentioned in Multiple Newspaper Articles (Referring to Chapter 4) (Continued)

Last Name	First Name	State	Year 1st Implicated	Senator *	Count
Pittman	Key	NV	1939	1	2
Powell	Adam	NY	1966	0	2
Rainey	Henry	IL	1932	0	2
Ray	George	NY	1900	0	2
Reed	Daniel	NY	1953	0	2
Rivers	Lucius	SC	1969	0	2
Rogers	John	AR	1890	0	2
Russell	Richard	GA	1959	1	2
Schafer	John Charles	WI	1929	0	2
Simpson	Alan	WY	1982	1	2
Stark	Fortney (Pete)	CA	2003	0	2
Stone	William	MO	1918	1	2
Sulzer	William	NY	1903	0	2
Thurman	Allen	OH	1879	1	2
Treadway	Allen	MA	1938	0	2
Tydings	Millard	MD	1948	1	2
Warren	Elizabeth	MA	2017	1	2
Wellington	George	MD	1902	1	2
Wheeler	Charles	KY	1902	0	2
Wherry	Kenneth	NE	1949	1	2
Wiley	Alexander	WI	1960	1	2
Williams	John James	DE	1963	1	2
Wright	Jim	TX	1988	0	2
Yoho	Ted	FL	2020	0	2

Source: Compiled by the author from newspaper reports in the *New York Times* and *Washington Post*.
* A "0" designates a member of the House of Representatives.

Appendix B

Table A.2 Sample of Topics Discussed in the *Congressional Digest*: 1921–2023 (Referring to Chapter 5)

Decade	Year	Month	Topic
1920s	1922	7	Ship subsidy bill
	1928	4	Limiting the tenure of presidents to two terms
	1929	8.5	Establishment of an international bank
1930s	1933	4	Revision of banking regulations to unify the system
	1938	4	Proposed sanctions and boycott of Japan
	1939	6.5	National Labor Relations Board
1940s	1945	10	Programs to reduce/eliminate unemployment
	1946	8.5	National health care
	1949	8.5	Direct election of the president of the United States
1950s	1951	5	Proposal to regulate executive branch propaganda
	1953	5	Revision of the Federal Lobbying Act
	1954	8.5	Trade policies with Communist bloc nations
1960s	1965	4	Continuation of current Vietnam policy
	1966	12	Proposal to change gun control laws
	1967	1	Federal standards for state unemployment compensation
1970s	1970	2	Creation of a Federal Insurance Guaranty Corporation
	1973	5	Freedom of the press protections
	1977	3	Federal financing of congressional election campaigns
1980s	1982	4	Curtail student aid
	1985	5	Economic development in distressed areas (Enterprise Zones)
	1987	12	Reform of the War Powers Act
1990s	1995	3	Eliminating unfunded mandates
	1995	5	Reform of the legal system (tort reform)
	1998	6.5	Drunk driving national standards
2000s	2000	5	Taxing e-commerce
	2002	3	Deregulation of high-speed Internet access
	2007	4	Funding for renewable energy and a clean energy future

(*continued*)

Table A.2 Sample of Topics Discussed in the Congressional Digest: 1921–2023 (Referring to Chapter 5) (Continued)

Decade	Year	Month	Topic
2010s	2013	10	Sexual assault in the military
	2016	1	Refugee resettlement laws
	2017	7	School choice including school vouchers and charter schools
2020s	2021	3	Immigration reform and detention facilities
	2022	1	Voting rights and new federal voting standards
	2022	8	Supreme Court reform and greater judicial ethics controls

Source: Compiled by the author from the *Congressional Digest* available at https://congressionaldigest.com/congressional-digest-in-print/ (last accessed January 15, 2024).

Note: In each Issue, editors of the *Digest* present the pros and cons of specific legislative actions.

References

Alexander, Brian. 2021. *A Social Theory of Congress: Legislative Norms in the Twenty-First Century*. Lanham, MD: Lexington Books.
American Political Science Association (APSA). 1950. "Summary of Conclusions and Proposals." *The American Political Science Review* 44(3): 1–14.
Bendix, William, and Jon MacKay. 2017. "Partisan Infighting among House Republicans: Leaders, Factions, and Networks of Interests." *Legislative Studies Quarterly* 42(4): 549–77.
Berkman, Michael. 1993. "Former State Legislators in the U.S. House of Representatives: Institutional and Policy Mastery." *Legislative Studies Quarterly* 18(1): 77–104.
Bernard, Jessie, T. H. Pear, Raymond Aron, and Robert C. Angell. 1957. *The Nature of Conflict*. Paris: Published by UNESCO.
Bertram, Wyatt-Brown. 1986. *Honor and Violence in the Old South*. New York: Oxford University Press.
Bessette, Joseph M. 1994. *The Mild Voice of Reason: Deliberative Democracy and American National Government*. Chicago, IL: University of Chicago Press.
Binder, Sarah. 1999. "The Dynamics of Legislative Gridlock, 1947-1996." *American Political Science Review* 93(3): 519–36.
Binder, Sarah. 2003. *Stalemate: Causes and Consequences of Legislative Gridlock*. Washington D.C.: Brookings Institute.
Binder, Sarah. 2017. "Legislating in Polarized Times." In *Congress Reconsidered*, 11th edition, eds. Lawrence C. Dodd and Bruce I. Oppenheimer. Thousand Oaks, CA: Sage Publishers, pp. 399–420.
Binder, Sarah A., and Forrest Maltzman. 2002. "Senatorial Delay in Confirming Federal Judges, 1947-1998." *American Journal of Political Science* 46(1): 190–99.
Blake, Robert. R., and Jane S. Mouton. 1964. *The Managerial Grid: Key Orientations for Achieving Production through People*. Houston, TX: Gulf Publishing Company.

Brady, David W. 1988. *Critical Elections and Congressional Policy Making*. Stanford, CA: Stanford University Press.

Bond, Jon R., and Richard Fleisher. 2000. *Polarized Politics: Congress and the President in a Partisan Era.* Washington, D.C.: Congressional Quarterly Press.

Boudon, Raymond. 1998. "Limitations of Rational Choice Theory." *American Journal of Sociology* 104(3): 817–28

Box-Steffensmeier, Janet M., Suzanna De Boef, and Tse-min Lin. 2004. "The Dynamics of the Partisan Gender Gap." *The American Political Science Review* 98(3): 515–28.

Budge, Ian, Hans-Dieter Klingemann, and Eric Tanenbaum. 2001. *Mapping Policy Preferences: Estimates for Parties, Electors and Governments 1945-1998*. Oxford: Oxford University Press.

Burden, Barry C., Gregory A. Caldeira, and Tim Groseclose. 2000. "Measuring the Ideologies of U.S. Senators: The Song Remains the Same." *Legislative Studies Quarterly* 25(2): 237–58.

Burns, James M. 1963. *The Deadlock of a Democracy*. Englewood Cliffs, CA: Prentice-Hall Publishers.

Cash, W. J. 1941. *The Mind of the South*. London: Penguin Books.

Christiano, Thomas. 2004. "Is Normative Rational Choice Theory Self-Defeating?" *Ethics* 115(1): 122–41.

Clinton, Joshua, and John Lapinski. 2006. "Measuring Legislative Accomplishment, 1877-1994." *American Journal of Political Science* 50(1): 232–49.

Clinton, Joshua, and John Lapinski. 2007. "Measuring Significant Legislation, 1877-1948." In *Party, Process, and Political Change in Congress*, Volume 2, eds. David Brady and Mathew McCubbins. Palo Alto, CA: Stanford University Press, pp. 361–78.

Cohen, Dov, Joseph Vandello, Sylvia Puente, and Adrian Rantilla. 1999. "When You Call Me That, Smile!" *Social Psychology Quarterly* 62(3): 257–75.

Coleman, John J. 1997. "The Decline and Resurgence of Congressional Party Conflict." *Journal of Politics* 59(1): 165–84.

Coleman, John J. 1999. "Unified Government, Divided Government, and Party Responsiveness." *American Political Science Review* 93(4): 821–35.

Conover, Pamela Johnston, and Virginia Sapiro. 1993. "Gender, Feminist Consciousness, and War." *American Journal of Political Science* 37(4): 1079–99.

Cook, Timothy E., and Paul Gronke. 2005. "The Skeptical American: Revisiting the Meanings of Trust in Government and Confidence in Institutions." *The Journal of Politics* 67(3): 784–803.

Cooper, Joseph. 1970. *The Origins of the Standing Committees and Development of the Modern House*. Houston, Texas: William Marsh Rice University.

Cooper, Joseph, ed. 1999. *Congress and the Decline of the Public Trust*. Boulder, CO: Westview Press.

Cooper, Joseph. 2017. "The Balance of Power between the Congress and the President: Issues and Dilemmas." In *Congress Reconsidered*, 11th Edition, eds. Lawrence C. Dodd and Bruce I. Oppenheimer. Thousand Oaks, CA: Sage Publications, pp. 357–98.

Cooper, Joseph, and David W. Brady. 1981. "Institutional Context and Leadership Style: The House from Cannon to Rayburn." *American Political Science Review* 75: 411–25.

Dahl, Robert. 1967. *Pluralist Democracy in the United States*. Chicago, Illinois: Rand McNally.

Dahl, Robert. 1971. *Polyarchy*. New Haven, Connecticut: Yale University Press.

De Dreu, Carsten K.W. 2008. "The Virtue and Vice of Workplace Conflict: Food for (Pessimistic) Thought." *Journal of Organizational Behavior* 29(1): 5–18.

De Neve, Jan-Emmanuel. 2015. "Personality, Childhood Experience, and Political Ideology." *Political Psychology* 36(1): 55–73.

Dodd, Lawrence C. 1981. "Congress, the Constitution, and the Crisis of Legitimation." In *Congress Reconsidered*, 2nd Edition, eds. Lawrence C. Dodd and Bruce I. Oppenheimer. Washington, D.C.: Congressional Quarterly Press, pp. 390–420.

Dodd, Lawrence C., and Scot Schraufnagel. 2013. "Party Polarization and Policy Productivity in Congress: From Harding to Obama." In *Congress Reconsidered*, 10th Edition, eds. Lawrence C. Dodd and Bruce I. Oppenheimer. Washington, D.C.: Sage/Congressional Quarterly Press, pp. 437–64.

Dodd, Lawrence C., and Scot Schraufnagel. 2009. "Congress, Civility and Legislative Productivity: A Historical Perspective." In *Congress Reconsidered*, 9th Edition, eds. Lawrence C. Dodd and Bruce I. Oppenheimer. Washington, D.C.: Congressional Quarterly Press. pp. 353–73.

Dodd, Lawrence C., and Scot Schraufnagel. 2012. "Congress and the Polarity Paradox: Party Polarization, Member Incivility and Landmark Legislation, 1891-1994." *Congress and the Presidency* 39(2): 109–32.

Dodd, Lawrence C., and Scot Schraufnagel. 2013a. "Taking Incivility Seriously: Analyzing Breaches of Decorum in the U. S. Congress (1891-2012)." In *Politics to the Extreme*, eds. Sean Q. Kelly and Scott A. Frisch. New York: Palgrave/MacMillan. pp. 71–92.

Dodd, Lawrence C., and Scot Schraufnagel. 2013b. "Party Polarization and Policy Productivity in Congress: From Harding to Obama." In *Congress Reconsidered*, 10th Edition, eds. Lawrence C. Dodd and Bruce I. Oppenheimer. Washington, D.C.: Sage/Congressional Quarterly Press. pp. 437–64.

Dodd, Lawrence C., and Scot Schraufnagel. 2017. "Party Polarization and Productivity in Congress." In *Congress Reconsidered*, 11th Edition. eds. Lawrence C. Dodd and Bruce I. Oppenheimer. Washington, D.C.: Sage/Congressional Quarterly Press, 207–36.

Edwards III, George C., Andrew Barrett, and Jeffrey Peake. 1997. "The Legislative Impact of Divided Government." *American Journal of Political Science* 41(2): 545–63.

Fenno, Richard F. 1997. *Learning To Govern. An Institutional View of the 104th Congress*. Washington, DC: Brookings Institution Press.

Fiorina, Morris. 1992. *Divided Government*. New York: MacMillan Publishing Company.

Friedrich, Carl Joachim. 1963. *The Philosophy of Law in Historical Perspective*. Chicago, IL: University of Chicago Press.

Frimer, Jeremy A., Harinder Aujla, Matthew Feinberg, Linda J. Shitka, Karl Aquino, Johannes C. Eichstaedt, and Robb Willer. 2022. "Incivility is Rising among American Politicians on Twitter." *Social Psychology and Personality Science* 14(2): 259–69.

Garand, James C. 2010. "Income Inequality, Party Polarization, and Roll-Call Voting in the U.S. Senate." *The Journal of Politics* 72(4): 1109–28.

Ginsberg, Benjamin. 1972. "Critical Elections and the Substance of Party Conflict: 1844-1968." *Midwest Journal of Political Science* 16: 603–25.

Goodwyn, Lawrence, 1978. *The Populist Movement: A Short History of the Agrarian Revolt in America.* Oxford: Oxford University Press.

Grant, Tobin J., and Nathan J. Kelly 2008. "Legislative Productivity of the U.S. Congress, 1789-2004." *Political Analysis* 16(3): 303–23.

Green, John C., John S. Jackson, and Nancy L. Clayton. 1999. "Issue Networks and Party Elites in 1996." In *The State of the Parties*, 3rd Edition, eds. John C. Green and Daniel M. Shea. Lanham, MD: Rowman and Littlefield, pp. 105–19.

Groseclose, Timothy, and Keith Krehbiel. 1994. "Golden Parachutes, Rubber Checks, and Strategic Retirements from the 102d House." *American Journal of Political Science* 38(1): 75–99.

Heitshusen, Valerie, and Garry Young. 2006. "Macropolitics and Changes in the U.S. Code: Testing Competing Theories of Policy Production, 1874-1946." In *Macropolitics of Congress*, eds. E. Scott Adler and John S. Lapinski. Princeton, NJ: Princeton University Press.

Hibbing, John R., and Elizabeth Theiss-Morse. 1995. *Congress as Public Enemy.* Cambridge: Cambridge University Press.

Hild, Matthew. 2007. "Agrarian Discontent and Political Dissent in the South, 1872–1882." In *Greenbackers, Knights of Labor, and Populists: Farmer-Labor Insurgency in the Late-Nineteenth-Century South*, 9–44. Athens, GA: University of Georgia Press.

Hindmoor, Andrew. 2011. "'Major Combat Operations Have Ended'? Arguing about Rational Choice." *British Journal of Political Science* 41(1): 191–210.

Hiroi, Taeko, and Lucio Renno. 2014. "Dimensions of Legislative Conflict: Coalitions, Obstructionism and Lawmaking in Multiparty Presidential Regimes." *Legislative Studies Quarterly* 39(3): 357–86.

Hixon, William A. and Aaron E. Wicks. 2000. "Measuring Congressional Support for the President: Evaluating NOMINATE Scores." *Presidential Studies Quarterly* 30(1): 186–202.

Hobbes, Thomas. 1991 [1651]. *Leviathan.* Edited by Richard Tuck. Cambridge: Cambridge University Press.

Holsti, Ole R., and James N. Rosenau. 1996. "Liberals, Populists, Libertarians, Conservatives: The Link between Domestic and International Affairs." *International Political Science Review* 17(1): 29–54.

Howell, William E., E. Scott Adler, Charles Cameron, and Charles Riemann. 2000. "Divided Government and the Legislative Productivity of Congress." *Legislative Studies Quarterly* 25(2): 285–312.

Hull Hoffer, William James. 2010. *The Caning of Charles Sumner: Honor, Idealism, and the Origins of the Civil War.* Baltimore, MD: John Hopkins University Press.

Hunt, James L. 2003. *Marion Butler and American Populism*. Chapel Hill, NC: University of North Carolina Press.

Inglehart, Ronald, and Pippa Norris. 2000. "The Developmental Theory of the Gender Gap: Women's and Men's Voting Behavior in Global Perspective." *International Political Science Review / Revue Internationale de Science Politique* 21(4): 441–63.

Iyengar, Shanto, Gaurav Sood, and Yphtach Lelkes. 2012. "Affect, Not Ideology: A Social Identity Perspective on Polarization." *Public Opinion Quarterly* 76(3): 405–31.

Jacobson, Gary C., and Michael A. Dimock. 1994. "Checking Out: The Effects of Bank Overdrafts on the 1992 House Elections." *American Journal of Political Science* 38(3): 601–24.

Jamieson, Kathleen Hall. 1992. *Dirty Politics: Deception, Distraction, and Democracy*. Oxford: Oxford University Press.

Jamieson, Kathleen Hall, and Falk, Erika. 2000. "Continuity and Change in Civility in the House." In *Polarized Politics: Congress and the President in a Partisan Era*, eds. John Bond and Richard Fleischer. Washington, DC: Congressional Quarterly Press, pp. 96–108.

Jehn, Karen A. 1995. "A Multimethod Examination of the Benefits and Determinants on Intragroup Conflict." *Administrative Science Quarterly* 40(2): 256–82.

Jehn, Karen A. 1997. "A Qualitative Analysis of Conflict Types and Dimensions in Organizational Groups." *Administrative Science Quarterly* 42(3): 530–57.

Jessee, Stephen, and Neil Malhotra. 2010. "Are Congressional Leaders Middlepersons or Extremists? Yes." *Legislative Studies Quarterly* 35(3): 361–92.

Jiang, Jane Yan, Xiao Zhang, and Dean Tjosvold. 2013. "Emotion Regulation as a Boundary Condition of the Relationship between Team Conflict and Performance: A Multi-Level Examination." *Journal of Organizational Behavior* 34(5): 714–34.

Jones, Charles O. 1994. *The Presidency in a Separated System*. Washington D.C.: Brookings Institute.

Jones, Bryan D., and Frank Baumgartner. 2005. *The Politics of Attention*. Chicago, IL: University of Chicago Press.66.

Kantrowitz, Stephen. 2016. *Tillman, Benjamin Ryan*. University of South Carolina, Institute for Southern Studies. https://www.scencyclopedia.org/sce/entries/tillman-benjamin-ryan/.

Kawato, Sadafumi. 1987. "Nationalization and Partisan Realignment in Congressional Elections." *American Political Science Review* 81(4): 1235–50.

Kelly, Sean Q. 1993. "Divided We Govern: A Reassessment." *Polity* 25(3): 475–84.

Kennedy, David M. 2009. "What the New Deal Did." *Political Science Quarterly* 124(2): 251–68.

Krehbiel, Keith. 1993. "Where's the Party?" *British Journal of Political Science* 23(2): 235–66.

Krehbiel, Keith. 1998. *Pivotal Politics: A Theory of U.S. Lawmaking*. Chicago: University of Chicago Press.

Lebo, Matthew J., Adam J. McGlynn, and Gregory Koger. 2007. "Strategic Party Government: Party Influence in Congress, 1789-2000." *American Journal of Political Science* 51(3): 464–81.

Likert, Rensis, and Jane Gibson Likert. 1976. *New Ways of Managing Conflict.* New York: McGraw-Hill Publishers.

Long. J. Scott. 1997. *Regression Models for Categorical and Limited Dependent Variables.* Thousand Oaks, CA: Sage Publications, Inc.

Loomis, Burdette, ed. 2000. *Esteemed Colleagues: Civility and Deliberation in the U. S. Senate.* Washington, DC: Brookings Institution Press.

Lopach, James J., and Jean A. Luckowski. 2005. *Jeannette Rankin: A Political Woman.* Boulder, CO: University Press of Colorado.

Lowell, A. Lawrence. 1902. "The Influence of Party upon Legislation in England and America." *Annual Report of the American Historical Association for 1901* 1: 319–542.

Luttig, Matthew D. 2017. "Authoritarianism and Affective Polarization: A New View on the Origins of Partisan Extremism." *The Public Opinion Quarterly* 81(4): 866–95.

Lyons, Jeffrey, Anand E. Sokhey, Scott D. McClurg, and Drew Seib. 2016. "Personality, Interpersonal Disagreement and Electoral Information." *The Journal of Politics* 78(3): 806–21.

Maass, Arthur. 1983. *Congress and the Common Good.* New York: Basic Books.

Machiavelli, Niccolo. 1998 [1532]. *The Prince.* Translated and Introduction by Harvey C. Mansfield. Chicago, IL: University of Chicago Press.

MacRae, Duncan, Jr. 1970. *Issues and Parties in Legislative Voting: Methods of Statistical Analysis.* New York: Harper & Row Publishers.

Malecki, Edward S. 1981. "The Capitalist State: Structural Variation and Its Implications for Radical Change." *The Western Political Quarterly* 34(2): 246–69.

Martin, Shannon E., and Kathleen A. Hansen. 1998. *Newspapers of Record in a Digital Age from Hot Type to Hot Links.* West Port, CT: Praeger Publishers.

Marx, Karl, and Friedrich Engels. 1998 [1848]. *The Communist Manifesto.* Edited by Mark Cowling, translated by Terrell Carver. Washington Square, NY: New York University Press.

Mann, Thomas E., and Norman J. Ornstein. 2006. *The Broken Branch: How Congress Is Failing America and How to Get It Back on Track* New York: Oxford University Press.

Maslin-Wicks, Kimberly. 2007. "Forsaking Transformational Leadership: Roscoe Conkling, the Great Senator from New York." *The Leadership Quarterly* 18(5): 463–76.

Mason, John Brown. 1938. "The State Legislature as Training for Further Public Service." *Annals of the American Academy of Political and Social Science* 195: 176–82.

Mason, Lilliana. 2016. "A Cross-Cutting Calm: How Social Sorting Drives Affective Polarization." *Public Opinion Quarterly* 80(Special Issue): 351–77.

Matthews, Donald R. 1959. "The Folkways of the United States Senate: Conformity to Group Norms and Legislative Effectiveness." *American Political Science Review* 53(4): 1064–89.

Mayhew, David R. 1991. *Divided We Govern: Party Control, Lawmaking, and Investigations, 1946-1990*. New Haven, CT: Yale University Press.

Mayhew, David R. 2000. *America's Congress*. New Haven, CT: Yale University Press.

Milkis, Sidney M. 2014. "Ideas, Institutions, and the New Deal Constitutional Order." *American Political Thought* 3(1): 167–76.

Mill, John Stuart. 2003 [1859]. *Utilitarianism and On Liberty*. Introduction my Mary Warnock. Malden, MA: Blackwell Publishing.

Miller, Michael G., and Joseph L. Sutherland. 2022. "The Effect of Gender on Interruptions at Congressional Hearings." *American Political Science Review* 117(1): 103–21.

Mondak, Jeffery J. 1995. "Competence, Integrity, and the Electoral Success of Congressional Incumbents." *The Journal of Politics* 57(4): 1043–69.

National Archives. https://www.archives.gov/milestone-documents/president-john-f-kennedys-inaugural-address (last accessed September 12, 2023).

Nisbett, Richard E., and Dov Cohen. 1996. *Culture of Honor: The Psychology of Violence in the South*. Boulder, CO: Westview Press.

Norrander, Barbara. 1997. "The Independence Gap and the Gender Gap." *The Public Opinion Quarterly* 61(3): 464–76.

Owens, John E., Scot Schraufnagel, and Quan Li. 2016. "Assessing the Effects of Personal Characteristics and Context on US House Speakers' Leadership Styles, 1789-2006." *Sage Open* 7(April–June): 1–14.

Park, Ju Yeon. 2021. "When Do Politicians Grandstand? Measuring Message Politics in Committee Hearings." *Journal of Politics* 83(1): 214–28.

Patterson, Samuel C., Gerhard Loewenberg, and Malcolm E. Jewell. 1983. "Editors' Introduction." *Legislative Studies Quarterly* 8(1): 1–4.

Pearson, Kathryn, and Eric Schickler. 2009. "Discharge Petitions, Agenda Control, and the Congressional Committee System, 1929–76." *The Journal of Politics* 71(4): 1238–56.

Peterson, Paul E., and Jay P. Greene. 1994. "Why Executive-Legislative Conflict in the United States Is Dwindling." *British Journal of Political Science* 24(1): 33–55.

Polsby, Nelson W. 1968. "The Institutionalization of the U.S. House of Representatives." *American Political Science Review* 62(1): 144–68.

Pondy, Louis R. 1967. "Organizational Conflict: Concepts and Models." *Administrative Science Quarterly* 12(2): 296–320.

Poole, Keith T. and Howard Rosenthal. 1997. *Congress: A Political-Economic History of Roll Call Voting*. New York: Oxford University Press.

Popkin, Samuel L. 2021. "*Crackup: the Republican Implosion and the Future of Presidential Politics*." New York: Oxford University Press.

Portteus, Kevin J. 2020. "My Beau Ideal of a Statesman": Abraham Lincoln's Eulogy on Henry Clay." *Journal of the Abraham Lincoln Association* 41(2): 1–24.

Quirk, Paul J. 1991. "Evaluating Congressional Reform: Deregulation Revisited." *Journal of Policy Analysis and Management* 10(3): 407–25.

Rice, Stuart A. 1928. *Quantitative Methods in Politics*. Norwood, MA: Lipton Press.

Roberts, Jason M., and Steven S. Smith. 2003. "Procedural Contexts, Party Strategy, and Conditional Party Voting in the U.S. House of Representatives, 1971-2000." *American Journal of Political Science* 47(2): 305–17.

Rogowski, Jon C., and Joseph L. Sutherland. 2016. "How Ideology Fuels Affective Polarization." *Political Behavior* 38(2): 485–508.

Rohde, David. 1991. *Parties and Leaders in the Postreform House.* Chicago, IL: University of Chicago Press.

Ross, Marc Howard. 1993. *The Culture of Conflict.* New Haven, CT: Yale University Press.

Sapiro, Virginia, and Pamela Johnston Conover. 1997. "The Variable Gender Basis of Electoral Politics: Gender and Context in the 1992 US Election." *British Journal of Political Science* 27(4): 497–523.

Schattschneider, E. E. 1960. *The Semi-Sovereign People: A Realist's View of Democracy in America.* New York: Holt, Rinehart, and Winston.

Schraufnagel, Scot D., and Jeffery J. Mondak. 2002. "The Issue Positions of Democrats and Republicans in the U.S. House, 1998: A Research Note." *Political Science Quarterly* 117(3): 479–90.

Schraufnagel, Scot. 2005. "Testing the Implications of Incivility in the United States Congress 1977-2000: The Case of Judicial Confirmation Delay." *Journal of Legislative Studies* 11(2): 216–34.

Schraufnagel, Scot. 2011. *Third Party Blues: The Truth and Consequences of Two-Party Dominance.* London: Routledge-Taylor Francis.

Shapiro, Robert Y. 2011. "Public Opinion and American Democracy." *The Public Opinion Quarterly* 75(5): 982–1017.

Shaw, Christopher W. 2020. "The Politics of Elite Anxiety: Carter Glass and American Financial Policy." *The Historian* 82(3): 308–27.

Sinclair, Barbara. 2000. "Individualism, Partisanship, and Cooperation in the Senate." In *Esteemed Colleagues: Civility and Deliberation in the U.S. Senate,* ed. Burdette Loomis. Washington, DC: Brookings Institution Press, pp. 59–77.

Sinclair, Barbara. 2006. *Party Wars: Polarization and the Politics of National Policy Making.* Norman, OK: University of Oklahoma Press.

Sindler, Allan P. 1956. *Huey Long's Louisiana: State Politics, 1920-1952.* Baltimore, MD: The John Hopkins Press.

Skocpol, Theda, and Lawrence R. Jacobs. 2011. "Reaching for a New Deal: Ambitious Governance, Economic Meltdown, and Polarized Politics." In *Reaching for a New Deal: Ambitious Governance, Economic Meltdown, and Polarized Politics in Obama's First Two Years,* eds. Theda Skocpol and Lawrence R. Jacobs. New York: Russell Sage Foundation, pp. 1–50.

Skultety, Steven. C. 2009. "Competition in the Best of Cities: Agonism and Aristotle's Politics." *Political Theory* 37(1): 44–68.

Skytte, Rasmus. 2020. "Dimensions of Elite Partisan Polarization: Disentangling the Effects of Incivility and Issue Polarization." *British Journal of Political Science* 51(4): 1–19.

Stimson, James A. 1991. *Public Opinion in America: Moods, Cycles, and Swings.* Boulder, CO: Westview Press.

Shaw, Jason D., Jing Zhu, Michelle K. Duffy, Kristin L. Scott. 2011. "A Contingency Model of Conflict and Team Effectiveness." *Journal of Applied Psychology* 96(2): 391–400.

Smith, Adam. 1985 [1776]. *An Inquiry into the Nature and Causes of the Wealth of Nations*. Introduction by Richard F. Teichgraeber III. New York, Random House Publishers.

St. Augustine. 1950 [426]. *The City of God*. Translation by Henry Bettenson. London: Penguin Books.

Stabile, Donald R. 1997. "Adam Smith and the Natural Wage: Sympathy, Subsistence and Social Distance." *Review of Social Economy* 55(3): 292–311.

Stone, Walter J., Ronald B. Rapoport, and Alan I. Abramowitz. 1999. "Party Polarization: The Reagan Revolution and Beyond." In *The Parties Respond*, ed. L. Sandy Maisel. Boulder, CO: Westview Press, pp.69–99.

Stonecash Jeffrey M. and Everita Silina. 2005. "The 1896 Realignment: A Reassessment." *American Politics Research* 33(1): 3–32.

Theriault, Sean. 2008. *Party Polarization in Congress*. Cambridge: Cambridge University Press.

Turner, Julius, and Edward V. Schneier, Jr. 1970. *Party and Constituency: Pressures on Congress*. Revised Edition. Baltimore, MD: John Hopkins University Press.

Uslaner, Eric M. 1993. *The Decline of Comity in Congress*. Ann Arbor, MI: The University of Michigan Press.

Uslaner, Eric M. 2000. "Is the Senate More Civil than the House?" In *Esteemed Colleagues: Civility and Deliberation in the U.S. Senate*, ed. Burdett A. Loomis. Washington DC: Brookings Institution Press, pp. 32–55.

Volden, Craig, and Alan Wiseman. 2018. "Legislative Effectiveness in the United States Senate." *Journal of Politics* 80(2): 731–35.

Weinschenk, Aaron C., and Christopher T. Dawes. 2017. "The Relationship between Genes, Personality Traits, and Political Interest." *Political Research Quarterly* 70(3): 467–79.

Wright, Gerald C., and Michael Berkman. 1986. "Candidates and Policy in United States Senate Elections." *American Political Science Review* 80(2): 567–88.

Yuan, Meng, and Scot Schraufnagel. 2019. "Two-dimensional Legislative Conflict: Unique Implications for the Effectiveness of Local Councils." *Local Government Studies* 46(5): 780–99.

Index

Page references for figures and tables are italicized

1st Congress, 36–37, 53, 77, 81, 88–89, 119
45th Congress, 21–22, 26, 31, *50, 52, 63*, 81, 89, 90
47th Congress, 31, 33, 48, 60, 66, 89
47th Senate, 31, 41n9
48th Congress, 31
51st Congress, 66
54th Congress, 66, 113
56th Congress, 66
57th Congress, 89
58th Congress, 87, 89
62nd Congress, 60, 66
65th Congress, 105
66th Congress, 53
67th Congress, 34, 73, 78, 86, 96
68th Congress, 75, 77–78
72nd Congress, 101
73rd Congress, 75, 91, 92, 104–5; Great Depression, 91, 98, 103–4
74th Congress, 24, 39
82nd Congress, 91
83rd Congress, 24–25, 39, 87
87th Congress, 78, 109
88th Congress, 89
89th Congress, 75, 89
91st Congress, 78
93rd Congress, 47, 89
94th Congress, 97
97th Congress, 37
102nd Congress, 11, 16n15, 92
103rd Congress, 37, 77, 81, 89, 91, 99
104th Congress, 48, 77
105th Congress, 89
106th Congress, 77
107th Congress, 22, 24, 44, 54
108th Congress, 44–47, 51, 90
111th Congress, 36, 104; Affordable Care Act (Obamacare), 36; Lily Ledbetter Fair Pay Act, 36
112th Congress, 91, 95; Great Recession, 91, 98, 103–4
113th Congress, 119
114th Congress, 26, 28, 40n3
115th Congress, 74–75, 122n22
116th Congress, 10, 22, 26, 31, 34, *50, 52, 63,* 67, 74, 77, 86, 95–97, 101, 119
117th Congress, 122n22
118th Congress, 10, 36–37, 67, 120

Adams, John Quincy (John Adams), 110–12, 114
affective polarization, 3–4, 8, 10, 118, 120
Aldrich, Nelson, 117

American Political Science Association (APSA), 34, 98, 108
Aristotle, ix
Arthur, Chester A., 31, 89
Augustine, St, ix
authoritarian, 3, 4, 57, 99

Berger, Victor, 48, 60
Biden, Joe (Joseph Biden), 10, 37
Boebert, Lauren, 10, 67
Boehner, Jon, 28
Bush, George W., 53
Byrd, Robert C., 8

Capitol Hill, 21
Carter, Jimmy, 31, 53
Civilian Conservation Corps, 24
civility norms, xi, 3–4, 12, 13, 15, 19–21, 24, 40n1, 45–46, 68, 107
Civil War, ix, 1, 17n16, 110, 112, 115; Post-Civil War, 72, 113, 116; Pre-Civil War, 72, 110, 111
Clay, Henry, 111–12, 114
Clinton, Bill, 37, 77, 89; North American Free Trade Agreement Implementation Act, 77; Violent Crime Control and Law Enforcement Act, 77
Clinton-Lapinski measure, 69, 72, 81, 86, 88–89, 91, 93, 99, 106nn2–3, 106n9
Colmer, William, 109
Congressional Digest (*Digest*), 73–75, *76*, 77–78, *79*, *80*, 81–82, 83n2, 85–86, 88–92, 93, 95–98, 100, 101, *102*, 105, 106n5
Conkling, Roscoe, 33, 115–16, 119
Constitutions, US, 5, 109
Cornyn, John, 119
Crank, Jeff, 47
Cruz, Ted (Rafael Edward Cruz), 10, 28, 115, 118–20, 122n20

Dahl, Robert, xii, 14–15, 33, 87
DeLay, Tom, 46
Democrat, 8–9, 28–29, 31, 44, 48, 108–9, 113, 118; House Democrats, 49; Senate Democrats, 49; Southern conservative Democratic Party, 14, 28, 33, 95, 108–9
dependent variables: count, 58, 60, 62, 65, 67; legislative accomplishment, 36–37, 69, 72, 81, 86, 88, 93, 99, *100*, 103, 106nn2–3, 106n9; multiple mentions, 58, 60–62
divided government/divided party control of government, 71–72, 77, 82, 83n2, 90, 104–5
Dornan, Robert, 8–9
Downey, Thomas, 8–9
DW-NOMINATE, 31, *32*, 37, 40, 45–48, *50*, 60, 64, 66, 111, 113

Electoral College, 1, 77
Engels, Friedrich, ix–x

face valid/face validity, 28, 54, 82
Fenton, Reuben, 115
filibuster/Senate filibuster, 33, 43, 87
Floyd, George, 1

Garfield, James A., 31, 89
Gilded Age, 112–13
Glass, Carter, 115, 117–18, 120; Glass-Steagall Act, 118
Goodwyn, Taylor, 114
Great Society Congresses, 28, 95
Greene, Marjorie Taylor, 10, 67
gridlock, 11, 13, *14*, 26, 40, 65, 72, *80*, 81, 84n5, 87, 98, 100, 103. *See also* stalemate

Halleck, Charles, 109
Hanna, Marcus, 66
Hefley, Joel Maurice (Joel Hefley), 44, 46, 47
Helms-Burton Act, 74
Hill, David, 66
Hobbes, Thomas, ix

Incidence Rate Ratios (IRR), 62, 65
independent variables: chair/committee chair, 59, 60, *63*, 65; female, 62, *63*,

65–67; leader/party leader, 59, 60, 63, 65; legislative experience/state legislator, 60–61, 63, 65–68, 111, 121; party maverick, 59, 60, 63, 64–66, 68; *passed House*, 92–93, *102*; *passed Senate*, 92–93, *102*; Southern, 61–62, 63, 64–65; time left, 92–93, 101, *102*
interactive two-dimensional conflict, 87, 92, 95, *96*

Johnson, Andrew, 115
Johnson, Lyndon, 36–37, 71, 77, 89, 109

Kennedy, John F., 31, 78, 89, 107, 109, 112
Kennedy, Robert P., 6

Lamar, Lucius Quintus, 116
legislative capacity, 91
Legislative Conflict Theory (LCT), xii, 2–4, 10, 15–16, 19, 21, 36–37, 39, 54, 69, 72, 78, 81–82, 83n2, 86–90, 92–93, 95–96, *96*, 99–101, 103, 105, 107, 111, 114–15, 119, 121; moderate conflict/moderate polarization/moderate legislative conflict, xii, 4, 6, 14–16, 19, 33, 39–40, 41n10, 68, 72, 85–86, 90, 92–93, 95–96, *97, 100, 102,* 104–5, 106nn6, 8, 108, 110; scope, 2; two-dimensional legislative conflict, xi–xii, 2, 4, 6, 11, 12, *14,* 15–16, 19, 26, 36, 41n10, 43, 47, 51, 54, 57, 72, 81, 95, 98, 100, 104, 107–8, 120–21
legislative productivity, xii, *14,* 15–16, 20, 36, 39, 41n10, 53, 54, 68–69, 71–73, 78, 82, 83nn1–2, 85, 87–90, *94,* 95, 99, 101, 103–5, 108, 111, 115, 117; landmark legislative productivity/landmark productivity, 14, 37, 72, 115, 117
Lincoln, Abraham, 112
Long, Huey, 24–25, 54, 57–59, 62, 65, 114
Louisiana, 24, 25

McCarthy, Joseph, 24, 54, 58–59, 87; Army-McCarthy hearings, 25
McConnell, Mitch, 10, 28, 119
Machiavelli, Niccolo, ix–x
McInnis, Scott (Stephen Scott Emory McInnis), 9, 44, 46; Hasan Family Foundation, 46
McKinley, William, 22, 53, 89
McLaurin, John L., 7, 8, 116
Mahone, William, 31, 48, 60
Marx, Karl, ix, x; conflict theory, x
moderate polarization, 40, 86, 92–93, 95, 99, 101, 103–4, 106n6
most similar case design, 48

New Deal, 31, 37, 53, 71, 77, 95, 109; post-New Deal, 91, 98, 103
New York Times/Times, 20–26, *27,* 29, 41n3, 44, 58, 66, 85, 109
Nixon, Richard, 47, 53, 78, 89, 108–9. *See also* 91st Congress
norm-center perspective, 13

Obama, Barack, 36, 74, 92
Ocasio-Cortez, Alexandria, 10
Packwood, Robert (Bob), 8–9
partisan actors, 3–4; co-partisan, 3, 25, 37, 60, 121; partisan opponents, 3–4, 11, 15
Pelosi, Nancy, 10
Pettigrew, Richard, 66
Platt, Thomas, 33
political party polarization/party system polarization, 3, 12, 15, 37, 40, 43–44, 48, 51, 54, 58, 68, 86, 103, 108, 115, 117–18; high party polarization, 3, 11–12, 14, 36, 37, 115–16; low party polarization, 14, 26, 37, 117; moderate party polarization, 33–34, *35,* 87, 93; party polarization, 3, 11, 13–15, 20, 24, 29, *30,* 31, 36, 37, 39, 40, 43, 47, 53–54, 82, 88, 103, 115, 119; two-party polarization, 87, 113
Populist Party, 113–14

presidential honeymoon Congresses/ honeymoon Congress, 37, 53, 77, 88–90, 98, 103–4, 105n2
Progressive Party, 48, 114
Putin, Vladimir, 45

quasi-divided government, 90, 104–5
Quay, Matthew Stanley, 6

Rangel, Charles, 44
Rankin, Jeannette, 67–68
Rational Choice Theory (RCT), xi–xii; descriptive, xi–xii, 2, 4; prescriptive, xi–xii, 2, 4, 105, 107
Rayburn, Sam, 109
Reagan, Ronald, 37, 45
regression: Logistic Regression/ Logit Regression, 62; Mixed-Effects Logistic Regression, 86; Ordinary Least Squares, 99; Poisson Regression, 62, 65–66; Prais-Winsten Regression, 86, 99
relational conflict, xi, 3, 6, 8–15, 19–22, 24–26, 28, 31, 33, 36–37, 39, 40n1, 43–44, 46–49, 51, *52*, 53–54, 58, 59, 61–62, *63,* 64–68, 82, 83n2, 87, 103, 112, 118–20; hyper-conflict, 10, 33, 36, 57, 66, 87, 107, 110–14, 121; incivility/incivilities, 3, 6, 11–15, 21, 22, 24–26, 28, 33, 37, 39, 40n1, 41n7, 43, 46–47, 49, 51, 53–54, 57–60, 81, 83n2, 87, 93, 98, 115–16, 118–20; inter-party, 10, 14, 16, 24, 26, *27*, 28, 33, 36–37, *38*, 39–40, 41n7, 54, 66, 87–88, 92, 93, 96, 98–99, 101–3; intra-party/ nonpartisan, 10, 16, 24–26, *27*, 28–29, 33, 36–37, 39, 40n3, 41n7, 54, 59, 67–68, 87, 93, 101, 108–10, 118, 120; legislative norm, xii, 6, 9; norm breaking, 3, 6, 10, 21, 26, 43–47, 54, 55, 58, 98, 114–16, 118–20; personalities/personal incivilities, 3, 5–6, 12, 21, 39, 45, 55, 66; two-dimensional inter-party conflict, 36, 92
Republican, 6–8, 10, 14, 16n14, 17n16, 28–29, 31, *32,* 33, 36–37, 44–49, 51, 64, 66–67, 95, 107, 109–10, 113–17, 119; lily white, 14, 17n16, 95; Republican House Freedom Caucus, 28; Southern conservative Republican Party, 28, 33, 109
Robinson, Joseph T., 24
Rohrabacher, Dana, 44–46
Roosevelt, Franklin D., 24, 37, 57–58, 77, 91
Roosevelt, Theodore, 89, 117

Senate majority size, 91, 98, 106n3
Senate moderation, 93
Senate polarization, 33, 39–40, 51, *52,* 87–88, 92–93, 95–96, 98–102
South Carolina, 7–8, 116–17
Southern society, 61; aristocratic political culture, 61
split partisan control, 104. *See also* quasi-divided government
Spooner, John Coit, 7
stalemate, 1, 40, 99, 105. *See also* gridlock
Stark, Peter (Pete Stark), 9, 44, 46
structural perspective, 13
Sumner, Charles, 116

task conflict, xi, 12–13
Thomas, Bill (William Marshall Thomas), 9, 44, 46
Tillman, Benjamin Ryan, 7, 59, 65, 115–17, 120, 122n14; Hepburn Rate Act, 117
Topical Legislative Productivity, xii, 34, 68, 73, 75, 77–78, *80,* 81, 83n2, 86, 88–89, 93, 95, *96, 97,* 101, *102,* 103, 105; landmark laws, 81, 83n2,

99, 105, 106n9; topical legislative success, 75
Trump, Donald (Donald J. Trump), 37, 73–75, 77–78
two-party dominant system, 98

unidimensional, 51, 64
unified government/unified party control, 77–78, 90, 98, 103–5

Vietnam War, 24

Washington Post/Post, 7, 20–27, *23, 27,* 40–41n3, 44, 58, 65, 116
Watergate, 24, 47, 110
Wilson, Woodrow, 53, 117–18
World War I, 67
World War II, 2, 22; Post-World War II, 20, 72, 74, 100; Pre-World War II, 91

About the Author

Professor Scot Schraufnagel is a former chair in the political science department at Northern Illinois University. In his twenties, he was a Peace Corps volunteer, serving in Sierra Leone, West Africa. He is the author or coauthor of six books, thirty journal articles, and numerous book chapters. National media outlets such as the *Washington Post*, the *New York Times*, *Politico*, and *CNN* have covered his research. His 2011 book *Third Party Blues: The Truth and Consequences of Two-Party Dominance* has received considerable scholarly attention and his coauthored book in 2018, *Historical Dictionary of the Barack Obama Administration,* won a Choice Award as an outstanding academic title from the U.S. Library of Congress. In his thirty years in the classroom, Dr. Schraufnagel has won recognition five times as an outstanding teacher, the first time in 1997 and most recently in 2023. Perhaps most importantly, Dr. Schraufnagel's students have gone on to successful careers as public servants at all levels of government, as attorneys, and as academics. He has coauthored publications with fifteen different students, helping to jump-start each student's professional career.